The World of Birds

The World of
Birds

Malcolm Ellis

Hamlyn
London New York Sydney Toronto

Published by THE HAMLYN PUBLISHING GROUP LIMITED
London · New York · Sydney · Toronto
Hamlyn House, Feltham, Middlesex, England
Copyright © The Hamlyn Publishing Group Limited 1971
Reprinted 1971

ISBN   0   600   03981   1

Printed in Italy by Arnoldo Mondadori Editore, Verona

Contents

How Birds
Have
Evolved

There can be few areas of the earth's surface that have not at some time been crossed by a bird, except perhaps for some parts of the Antarctic continent. Birds, like mammals, are warm-blooded creatures, and because they are not dependent upon the temperature of their environment, they are able to lead a very active life in widely differing habitats. A unique feature which sets them apart from all other animals is the fact that they have feathers. The possession of feathers not only helps them to regulate their body temperature, but also plays a major role in the ability of many of them to fly.

The earliest creature resembling present day birds known to man is *Archaeopteryx,* from the late Jurassic period, between 130 and 140 million years ago. The first evidence of the existence of this creature came from some fossils discovered in a limestone quarry in Bavaria in 1861. First, the imprint of a feather was found, clearly and distinctly marked on both sides of a slab of stone when it was split open, and then later the same year a skeleton was discovered. The remains of this specimen, which was named *Archaeopteryx lithographica,* were acquired by the British Museum (Natural History) in London. A second specimen was discovered in 1877, about ten miles away from where the first was found, and a third was found in the same locality in 1956. At one time the second *Archaeopteryx* was thought to be of a different species from the specimen preserved in London, but the smaller size and minor differences are now attributed to immaturity or difference of sex, or perhaps both.

Archaeopteryx was about the size of a magpie and combined the characteristics of a bird and reptile. By far the most important avian feature of this creature is that it possessed feathers, identical in structure with those of modern birds and similarly arranged on the forelimb or wing. Despite the well developed flight feathers, it had no keel on its breastbone, so could not have had very powerful flying muscles. It was probably capable only of gliding flight. The structure of its feet indicates that it was able to grasp branches, making it likely that it lived in trees. With the aid of the three claws it had on the bend of the wing, it was probably able to climb into the uppermost branches of trees and launch itself off and glide from one to another.

It differed from modern birds principally in having teeth in its bill, in retaining functional claws on the wing, and in having a long tail with vertebrae right down to the tip. The tail, which was as long as the body, had feathers in pairs on each side. None of its bones was hollow, a device developed in modern birds to keep down their weight, and already present in the reptilian flying pterosaurs. If *Archaeopteryx* had been discovered without the imprint of its feathers, it would doubtless have been classified as a reptile. The feathers prove that *Archaeopteryx* was a bird, however simple, and distinguish it from other animals.

There can be very little doubt that birds are descended from reptiles. The structure of *Archaeopteryx* points to the fact that it was a very important evolutionary link between reptiles and modern birds. *Archaeopteryx* probably descended from a long-tailed, lizard-like reptile that walked and ran

A reconstruction of *Archaeopteryx lithographica.* With the help of the three claws on each wing, it was probably able to climb about in the tops of trees and glide from one to another.

The fossilized remains of *Archaeopteryx lithographica* showing the imprint of the feathers

mainly on its hind legs, using its tail as a balancer and with its forearms free. Such a creature very probably belonged to a group of small, biped reptiles called *Pseudosuchia,* which lived in the previous Triassic geological period.

The long history of birds probably started when some of this group became attracted to life in the trees, perhaps to escape enemies, or perhaps to exploit a new source of food. Once well established in the trees, they probably started to jump from branch to branch and later from tree to tree. In living reptiles and mammals, such as flying squirrels, this is often aided by a flap of skin along the sides of the body to extend their jump and cushion the landing. Similarly, the arboreal reptile may have extended its arms as it jumped, and gradually enlarged scales were developed along the arms which in time evolved into feathers. Chemically, the composition of scales and feathers is similar.

Professor Pierce Brodkorb, an expert on fossil birds, has estimated that somewhere between one and a half and two million species of birds have existed at one time or another since *Archaeopteryx.* The prominent ornithologist, James Fisher, believes that the number is more likely to be less than half a million.

In spite of the early discovery of *Archaeopteryx,* there is a gap of some thirty million years before the Cretaceous period, when the next fossil evidence of birds is available. Being so light and fragile, unless bird remains fell into sedimentary deposits of gently running water, or quiet lakes or seas, they were unlikely to be preserved by fossilization. *Archaeopteryx* was preserved in a fine slate, formed from silt deposited at the bottom of a Bavarian lake. Birds that died on land, like their counterparts today, were eaten by scavengers or rapidly decomposed. The number of reasonably complete skeletons of birds that have been found is quite small in comparison to the amount of material of most other vertebrate classes. Accurate identification of many bird fossils is uncertain. Sometimes entire groups have been set up on the basis of very scanty evidence.

The evolution of birds was slow in their early years, and from the whole of the mild, long Cretaceous period, from about 135 to 70 million years ago, less than thirty species are known. Almost all the remains from this time belong to water birds. Throughout this period the dinosaurs continued to dominate the land. *Gallornis,* a goose- or flamingo-like bird described in 1931 from Lower Cretaceous beds in France, is the next oldest fossil after *Archaeopteryx* to be catalogued with certainty as a bird. It was identified from a thigh bone.

Best documented of the birds from these times are *Ichthyornis* and *Hesperornis* from the chalk beds of Kansas, which were once a seabed hundreds of miles from land. Over this sea that covered what is now Kansas soared a huge flying reptile, *Pteranodon,* which was the largest animal ever known to have flown. *Pteranodon,* which became extinct at the end of the Cretaceous period, possessed enormous bat-like wings with a span reaching twenty-seven feet.

Ichthyornis ('fish-bird') was superficially rather like a gull or tern in appearance, and stood about eight inches in height. It is known from a small number of

Hesperornis regalis from the chalk beds of Kansas was about 4 ft long; it is now thought that this bird may not have been toothed

Diatryma steini, a large carnivorous running bird from the Eocene of Wyoming; it stood about 7 ft high when erect

species, most of which are founded on scant material, except for the almost complete skeleton of *Ichthyornis victor*. The skeleton is not very different from that of a modern bird and shows a strong keel on the breastbone, indicating that it must have been able to fly well. *Ichthyornis* was for a long time thought to have possessed a toothed jaw, but recent research suggests that this was not so.

Hesperornis ('western bird') is known from several skeletons, which reveal that it was completely flightless. Perhaps five feet or more long from bill to tail, with strong legs and paddle-like feet, *Hesperornis* was doubtless adept at swimming and diving. Its legs were placed so far back on the body that they could have been of very little use on land. *Hesperornis* probably resembled a huge diver or loon.

With the beginning of the Tertiary period some seventy million years ago, the great reptiles had died out and birds and mammals were becoming dominant. In addition the Atlantic and Indian Oceans had been formed. The first part of the Tertiary period, usually called the Paleocene, produced very few fossil birds. With the coming of the Eocene, however, birds had really begun to radiate all over the world and many modern families evolved. These include not only penguins and early waterfowl, but some of the earlier hawks and vultures, as well as cranes and rails. *Diatryma,* a huge, flightless giant nearly seven feet tall, appeared and vanished in the Eocene. It had long legs which were well suited to running on the ground and a large head, armed with a powerful bill.

A time of orderly advancing development towards recent types took place during the Oligocene, which lasted from about forty to twenty-five million years ago. It was a warm time when mountains were formed and grasslands increased as the forests receded. A large number of fossil birds from these times have been unearthed in southern central France, including the first known storks, cuckoo, swift, trogons and Secretary Bird. Neither the Secretary Bird nor the trogons now occur in Europe. The fossil remains of a primitive trogon from Oligocene deposits in France suggest that the trogons once had a wider and more continuous distribution than they have today. Now they only occur in the warmer parts of the New World, Africa south of the Sahara, and from India eastwards to the Philippines and south to Indonesia. The Secretary Bird is confined to Africa. Divers, grebes and albatrosses also seem to date from this time.

After the Oligocene came the Miocene, which lasted until eleven million years ago; pelicans, storm petrels, pigeons and wagtails all originate from this warm period. The cooler Pliocene followed leading into the Pleistocene when there were four Ice Ages, the last of which occurred no more than 10,000 years ago. The Ice Ages had a profound effect on plants and animals, reducing the number of their species. Most Pleistocene birds are of species which still survive.

During the changes in the earth's surface, thousands of animals, many of them great mammals now extinct, became trapped in the tar-pits of Rancho la Brea in California. Of the many bird remains discovered, a large number belong to vultures and other birds of prey which came to feed on the carcasses of these unfortunate animals and were in

A Slavonian Grebe, a member of one of the primitive groups of water birds dating from the Oligocene

The Andean Condor with a wing-span of 9–10 ft is now the largest living bird of prey

The Woodpecker Finch is unique in using a cactus spine or twig as a tool for probing for insects

Dinornis maximus. The moas once inhabited New Zealand and the largest is estimated to have been a giant 10 ft high.

turn trapped themselves. Among the birds unearthed was a gigantic vulture, *Teratornis merriami*, an ancestor of the California Condor (*Gymnogyps californianus*). A careful study of the remains of this gigantic creature indicates that it weighed about fifty pounds and had a wing-span of perhaps fourteen feet; an even larger allied species, *Teratornis incredibilis,* which lived at about the same time, may have had a wing-span of seventeen feet. The Andean Condor (*Vultur gryphus*), the largest living bird of prey, has a wing-span of nine to ten feet and weighs about twenty-two to twenty-eight pounds.

The process of evolution is as important in understanding the birds of today as it is in understanding the birds of the past. Evolution can best be seen in actual progress in small isolated populations, where changes have the best chance of surviving. Examples of changes occurring from isolation are very well demonstrated by birds living on groups of islands separated by vast distances of water from the nearest mainland.

On the Galapagos Islands and Cocos Island in the Pacific Ocean, 600 miles off the west coast of South America, live a group of birds collectively known as Darwin's finches (*Geospizinae*). There are about thirteeen species, all similar enough to one another to show an obvious relationship, yet each markedly different. These birds are of great historical interest, for when Charles Darwin studied them during a visit by the 'Beagle' to the Galagapos Islands, they were instrumental in convincing him of the validity of his theory of evolution. Their nearest relatives, which came from the American mainland, are not known but are presumed to have been finches.

Darwin's finches are an outstanding example of adaptive radiation: the process whereby the descendants of related forms diverge in ways that enable them to exploit different ecological niches. The chief differences between these birds is in their bills, which vary from being stout and finch-like to long and thin like that of a warbler. Some have small, tit-like bills, while one has a parrot-like bill and another is down-curved. The different-shaped bills enable these otherwise similar birds to feed on a wide variety of foods. One, the Woodpecker Finch (*Camarhynchus pallidus*), has developed a unique habit. Breaking off a twig or picking up a cactus spine, it holds it in its bill and uses it as a tool for probing for insects, usually among the bark of trees.

Particularly on some of the smaller islands where there are fewer species, some of the finches have bills intermediate between those of species on larger islands. Despite the wide differences in their bills and modes of feeding, studies of their internal anatomy reveal the close relationship of the Darwin's finches to each other; a further indication is their breeding habits, which are remarkably similar for a group with such diverse methods of feeding.

The only other group at all comparable with Darwin's finches are the Hawaiian honeycreepers. This group of birds confined to the Hawaiian Islands have evolved much further than Darwin's finches, and exhibit an ever wider variety of bill adaptations, but fewer transitional forms survive. Early ornithologists were so impressed with the great diversity of bills and colours of the honeycreepers that they classified them as representatives of four families and eighteen genera. Diverse as they are in bill structure and colour, however, they have many similarities. Today, of the twenty-two species known, eight have already disappeared, and the remainder are almost wholly in danger of extinction. Having become so specialized, they have been unable to adapt themselves to the changes in their habitat caused by man, or to withstand the competition from other birds introduced by him. Like Darwin's finches, their nearest relatives, which are unknown, came from the American mainland.

Today's flightless birds are probably all descended from birds which once flew. The Ostrich, rheas, cassowaries, Emu and kiwis, which all lack a keel on their breastbone and are known as ratites, probably lost their powers of flight many millions of years ago. Except for the kiwis, the ratites all developed long legs for fast running, often on islands or continents with few or no predators likely to prey on them. Instead of relying on fleetness of foot for safety, the kiwis probably became nocturnal. Another group of flightless birds, the penguins, simply substituted water for air and turned their wings into flippers.

Aepyornis maximus. The elephant birds were large, flightless running birds like the moas and the largest may have weighed just under half a ton.

Their breastbone retains a keel to anchor the muscles which power their highly functional forelimbs.

The giant moas and elephant birds are two groups of ratites which are now extinct. The moas, which inhabited New Zealand, were well known to the Maoris, and probably vanished in comparatively recent times. *Dinornis maximus,* the largest, is estimated to have towered ten feet or more above the ground. Of the approximately twenty species, there is speculation that at least one of the smaller moas still survived into the early part of the nineteenth century. Although the moas were probably most closely related to the kiwis, they are thought to have resembled huge Emus in appearance.

Elephant birds lived in Madagascar, now called Malagasy, and were large, flightless running birds like the moas. Remains have been found in deposits dating from the Pleistocene to geologically recent times. *Aepyornis titan* stood about as tall as *Dinornis maximus,* and may have weighed a little less than half a ton, looking rather like an Ostrich on a gigantic scale. Eggs belonging to elephant birds have been found which have been estimated to have had a liquid content of two gallons and are the largest single animal cell known. The bones unearthed indicate that there were several species.

Since *Archaeopteryx* some 130 to 140 million years back in the Jurassic period, or perhaps even earlier, birds have slowly evolved from lizard-like creatures to the modern birds with which we are so familiar today. Modern birds are classified into twenty-seven orders, or main groups, comprising 154 families or smaller groupings. The ratites are regarded as being the most primitive, followed by the tinamous, which are probably most akin to the rheas. Next come the penguins, then the divers or loons, followed by the grebes.

There are eighteen other orders before the Passeriformes, the final and most highly developed order of birds. Included in this order are more than half of all the species of birds and more than one third of the recognized families. They are commonly known as passerines or perching birds. Their perching feet, with four unwebbed toes joined at the same level, three pointing forward and one back, are among their most characteristic features. Passerines are land birds that are found almost throughout the world, being absent only from the polar latitudes and a few oceanic islands. Most of them are highly successful, and have been able to adapt to living alongside man, often inhabiting cultivated land and gardens, and roosting or nesting on buildings. A very good example is the Common Starling (*Sturnus vulgaris*) which occurs in Britain and is also found across Europe, the Middle East, and much of Asia. In places where this species has been introduced, notably North America, it has increased rapidly because of its adaptability and aggressiveness, usually driving away native species. In addition, the group contains all the most accomplished songsters – and the best vocal mimics. The largest passerines are the ravens and lyrebirds. Because of their mode of life and the fragility of their skeletons, very few passerines became fossilized; in any case most of them are probably of very modern development.

The Distribution of the World's Birds

There are probably between 8,548 and 8,809 different species or kinds of birds in the world today. To arrive at an exact figure is difficult, for the individual opinions of the experts vary as to the status of certain forms. They range in size from the huge, flightless Ostrich (*Struthio camelus*) which may stand almost eight feet tall, to the diminutive Bee Hummingbird (*Mellisuga helenae*) of Cuba which has a total length of little more than two inches, half of which is accounted for by the bill and tail. Relatively few birds are cosmopolitan in their distribution; each species is associated with a definite area of the world within which, under normal circumstances, its population is confined. This may be an entire continent or more, or it may be an area of only a few square miles. Differences between fauna tend to be more pronounced where a physical barrier of some sort prevents animals from extending their range. Large oceans, deserts and mountain ranges form such barriers. It was largely from the study of birds that the ornithologist P. L. Sclater in 1858 divided the world's surface into what are known as zoogeographical regions. With some modifications, these regions are still employed to the present time, and form a useful and convenient starting point when considering the distribution of the world's birds.

In terms of the number and diversity of species, the richest of these regions is the Neotropical, which occupies Central America southwards from southern Mexico, South America, and the West Indies. About half the species of the world breed in this region, or visit it during the northern winter. Over 1,700 species have been recorded from Colombia, more than twice as many as have been recorded from North America. Many of the birds found in the Neotropical region, such as the macaws and other parrots, toucans, tanagers, and hummingbirds, are among the world's most colourful species.

The rheas are just one of the many groups that are unique to the region. Darwin's Rhea (*Pterocnemia pennata*) and the Common Rhea (*Rhea americana*), which show a general resemblance to the Ostrich, inhabit South America. Like the Ostrich they are flightless and are fine runners living in open country, but unlike the Ostrich, which has only two toes on each foot, they have three. The Common Rhea which is the larger of the two species, stands about five feet high and may weigh anything between forty-four and fifty-five pounds.

Also peculiar to the region is the Hoatzin (*Opisthocomus hoazin*), one of the strangest of all living birds. In many ways it is unique, for in some respects it is very primitive and in others very advanced. Measuring a little over two feet in length, it has a small head with an erect crest, large wings and a long broad tail. The plumage is mainly dark brown, with some reddish-brown and pale reddish-yellow, and there is bare blue skin around the eye. Hoatzins live along the overgrown banks of big rivers and their tributaries in northern South America from Guyana and Brazil to Colombia and Bolivia. They feed in flocks, usually of ten to twenty birds, on the tough leaves, flowers and fruits of certain marshy plants. Occasionally they also eat small animals, including fish and small crabs, which

A flock of Budgerigars arrive at a water-hole in their native Australia

Lesser and Greater Flamingos on Lake Nakuru, Kenya; all flamingos are highly gregarious and sometimes form huge flocks

17

top
Rheas are polygamous and the males
undertake most of the domestic chores,
each cock incubating the eggs of his five
or six hens and raising
the chicks alone

above
A male Ostrich with two Grant's Gazelle
grazing in the background

right
A close-up of the head of an Ostrich,
the largest of all living birds

they capture in the mud or shallow water under the vegetation. The Hoatzin has a most peculiar digestive system: unlike other birds that feed on a similar diet where the food is broken down in the gizzard, in this species the function is performed by a much enlarged crop. The crop is high in the chest, and after a large meal, it makes the Hoatzin top-heavy. To help preserve its balance when perching, the Hoatzin supports itself on its breastbone, which is covered by a special callosity or pad of horny skin. The wing structure of the young bird recalls that of *Archaeopteryx,* for there are two claws on each wing which can be moved by special muscles. As they grow up the young Hoatzins lose these claws, but still use their wings to help them climb among the foliage.

The jacamars and motmots found only in this region resemble the Old World bee-eaters in general appearance and many of their habits. Most of the fifteen or so species of jacamars have glittering metallic plumage in which greens, blues and bronzes predominate, and because of their long thin bills and brilliant iridescent colouring, are sometimes likened to overgrown hummingbirds. They are confined to wooded habitats, from southern Mexico southwards through Central America and the Amazon area to southern Brazil. Jacamars live exclusively on insects which they usually catch on the wing; blue morpho and large swallow-tailed butterflies are particular favourites. The eight species of motmots, which range from northern Central America to northern Argentina, are generally bigger than the jacamars. A characteristic feature of the more typical species is the tail with its two long central feathers which are bare for part of their length, and have a racquet-like tip. The two long tail feathers are fully feathered when they first grow, but a few weeks later part of the feathering falls away, aided by preening on the part of the motmot. Largest of the motmots is the Rufous Motmot (*Baryphthengus ruficapillus*) which measures eighteen inches in length, and is found from Nicaragua to Amazonia.

Seed-snipes, a purely South American family, are relatives of the waders which, in spite of their name, they do not closely resemble, for they have stout conical bills and short legs with small feet. Though they eat some insects, together with tender shoots and leaves, they are essentially seed-eaters. They have a zig-zag flight like the Common Snipe (*Gallinago gallinago*), and it is from this, as well as from their diet, that their name derives. There are four species which inhabit a variety of places from the Andean snowline to sandy and barren stretches of coastline. The largest is the White-bellied Seed-snipe (*Attagis malouinus*), which inhabits the southern parts of Argentina and Chile, including the island of Tierra del Fuego, and also the Falkland Islands.

Next in variety to the Neotropical region is the Ethiopian region, encompassing all of Africa south of the Sahara and the south-west corner of Arabia. The parts of Africa north of the Sahara belong to the Palaearctic region, the avifauna being more akin to southern Europe than Africa proper. It is interesting to note that the Sahara Desert rather than the Mediterranean Sea is a barrier to many species.

The best-known African bird is the Ostrich (*Struthio camelus*), a species which is not confined to the region, for it also occurs in North Africa and perhaps a small part of Arabia. The Ostrich was formerly abundant in North Africa and Arabia, but hunting with high-powered rifles from fast motor vehicles has driven it to the point of extinction in these areas. The Ostrich is the largest of all living birds. Adult males may stand nearly eight feet tall and weigh more than 300 pounds; females are slightly smaller. Ostriches usually travel about in pairs or small parties and are very wary and difficult to approach. Contrary to popular belief, they do not bury their heads in sand; they do, however, feed on the ground and when seen from a distance may appear to have their heads buried.

Other birds particularly characteristic of this region include the Secretary Bird (*Sagittarius serpentarius*), the Hammerhead (*Scopus umbretta*), mousebirds or colies, turacos, guinea fowl, oxpeckers, and wood hoopoes. The Ethiopian region is also rich is such groups as bustards, barbets, honeyguides, larks, shrikes, weavers and waxbills. On the other hand, certain groups, especially the parrots and woodpeckers, are represented by fewer species than might be expected.

The Secretary Bird is a bird of prey with long

The Golden-fronted Leafbird is a member of the only family peculiar to the Oriental region and is often exported as a cage-bird

The Blue-necked Tanager. There are about 200 species in this New World family which is mostly concentrated in Central and South America.

Most colourful of the macaws is the Scarlet Macaw, a bird found in the New World from Mexico south to Bolivia

The Ruby-throated Hummingbird is a
well-known summer visitor to eastern
North America and extends its range
as far north as southern Canada

The Hammerhead or Hammerkop is a
dull brown-coloured bird
found only in Africa south of the Sahara,
Malagasy, and south-western Arabia

A group of Vulturine Guineafowl, so named
because of the somewhat vulture-like
greyish-blue skin of their head and neck

A Red-throated Diver on its nest;
in North America this bird is known
as a loon

stilt-like legs found only in Africa. Its name originates from a reputed resemblance between its long crest feathers and the old-fashioned quill pens which secretaries and clerks used to place behind their ears. The stately Secretary Bird seeks its prey of reptiles, rats, mice and insects on open plains. Snakes are a favourite food and, like other prey, are killed by blows from the bird's feet.

Oxpeckers spend much of their time climbing about the hides of the larger African mammals and domestic stock in search of ticks, just as a woodpecker climbs tree trunks in search of insects. Only elephants and hippopotamuses do not seem to tolerate them. There are two species, the Yellow-billed Oxpecker (*Buphagus africanus*), although the end half of its bill is in fact red, and the Red-billed Oxpecker (*Buphagus erythrorhynchus*); the former is the most widely distributed, but occasionally birds of both species are seen on the same animal. Related to the starlings, oxpeckers are also known as tick birds and rhinoceros birds. It may be that it is not so much the ticks themselves that provide the birds' main food, as the blood with which they are gorged. Also, they will often remove ticks, and then suck blood from the open wound. Some people feel that they do good by removing many parasites that are often carriers of disease, while others feel that this is outweighed by the harm they do in preventing sores and wounds from healing.

Deep in the forests of the Congo lives the Congo Peacock (*Afropavo congensis*), a bird not described until as recently as 1936. Even then, its existence would not have been suspected had it not been for the sharp eyes of an American ornithologist who spotted an unidentified wing feather of a large bird in the head-dress of a pygmy tribesman. Following up this slender clue, he eventually discovered the living bird. It is the only African representative of the large tribe of pheasants and peafowl, so common and widespread in the Asian mainland and islands.

Despite the close proximity of Malagasy, many of the birds found on the African mainland do not occur there, while a number of the birds found in Malagasy are unique to the island. Along with its neighbouring islands, Malagasy is usually treated as a minor region additional to the major zoogeographical regions of the world. Among the birds not found elsewhere are a group of a dozen species known as vangas, which seem to replace the shrikes which are common in Africa. Another group are the two asities and two false sunbirds. The Wattled False Sunbird (*Neodrepanis coruscans*) was for many years considered to be a true sunbird as it resembles them so closely and lives and feeds in exactly the same way. Later research revealed, however, that certain anatomical characteristics which the false sunbirds share with the asities make it probable that both evolved from a common ancestor even though they are now quite different in appearance and habits.

The Australasian region extends from eastern Indonesia eastwards to New Guinea, Australia, New Zealand and Polynesia. Among the birds especially representative of this region are the Emu (*Dromaius novaehollandiae*), cassowaries, megapodes, lyrebirds, birds of paradise, and bowerbirds. New Zealand, where the giant moas flourished until historical times, is sometimes treated as a sub-region of the Australasian region. Some people have suggested that the kiwis may be related to the extinct moas. There are three species of kiwis, all of them peculiar to New Zealand.

Second in size only to the Ostrich, the Emu occurs over much of Australia, except for the tropical north-eastern corner, where it is replaced by the Australian Cassowary (*Casuarius casuarius*). The Emu may stand six feet tall and weigh 100 pounds. There is just one species of Emu, while there are three species of cassowaries. Apart from north-eastern Australia, cassowaries inhabit New Guinea and its adjacent islands. A distinctive feature of these birds is the bony helmet or casque on the top of the head which wards off obstructions as they run through thick undergrowth. The skin of their unfeathered heads and necks combines bright reds, blues, purples and yellow, and two species have decorative wattles hanging from their necks. They have stout, powerful legs, and the innermost of the three toes is armed with a long sharp claw. In combat, the cassowary leaps feet first at its adversary: there are many records of their killing humans when cornered.

The two species of lyrebirds, the Superb Lyrebird (*Menura novaehollandiae*) and the slightly smaller Albert's Lyrebird (*Menura alberti*), are restricted to eastern Australia and have no near relatives anywhere. The latter, which takes its name from Prince Albert, Queen Victoria's consort, has the more northerly range, being confined to a small area of rain forest in north-east New South Wales and south-east Queensland. The first specimens of lyrebirds were caught in 1798 about sixty miles south-west of Sydney and at that time were thought to be a type of pheasant or perhaps a bird of paradise. Most famous of the lyrebird's attributes is their extraordinary skill as mimics. The males also have a very elaborate display which is discussed in a later chapter on courtship, as is the display of the birds of paradise and bowerbirds, two other groups confined to this region.

The Oriental region comprises tropical Asia and western Indonesia. It stretches eastwards from a little west of India, and in the east includes the islands of Taiwan and Hainan. In the north, the main barrier separating it from the Palaearctic region is the Himalayas. Also included in this region, which extends as far east as Timor, are most of the Indonesian Archipelago, the Philippines, Borneo and the Celebes, as well as the Greater and Lesser Sunda Islands.

The leafbirds are the only family of birds peculiar to the Oriental region. Most strikingly plumaged of the group are the two species of fairy bluebirds (*Irena* spp.), the males of which are clad in light iridescent blue and velvety black; the eye is ruby red. All leafbirds are fine songsters and two species in particular, the Golden-fronted Leafbird (*Chloropsis aurifrons*) and the Orange-bellied Leafbird (*Chloropsis hardwickii*), are frequently kept as cage-birds for this reason, in Europe and the U.S.A. as well as in the East.

Sometimes the Palaearctic and Nearctic regions

A male Congo Peacock, the only large pheasant to have been found in Africa

Oxpeckers clustered on the back of a zebra

A group of Emus. This is a species which is
widespread in Australia where it is usually
considered a pest because it grazes the
grass wanted for sheep and also eats grain.

In tropical north-eastern Australia,
the Australian Cassowary replaces the Emu

are combined as the Holarctic region. The two regions have many avifaunal similarities, although there are also differences. Both are characterized by fewer species and by extensive annual migrations of birds during the northern winter. The Palaearctic region comprises the whole of Europe, Africa north of the Sahara, and Asia north of the Himalayas, while the Nearctic region consists of North America above the tropics. Especially representative of the Holarctic are the divers, grouse, phalaropes, and auks.

The divers, or loons as they are known in North America, are a primitive group of northern water birds. The four living species are the only birds whose legs are encased in the body right down to the ankle joint. The legs are set very far back and although their strong, propeller-like feet greatly enhance their skill in the water, they make the birds almost helpless on land, where they are scarcely able to walk. Normally, they come to land only to nest. The divers' superb diving ability has given rise to their common British name; there is even a record of one having been caught by a fisherman at a depth of 240 feet below the surface.

There are about eighteen species in the grouse family, and they differ from other gallinaceous birds in various ways; for example, their nostrils are hidden by feathers, and their legs are partly or fully feathered, no doubt as an adaptation to the hard winters most of them have to endure. One species, the Red Grouse (*Lagopus scoticus*), is restricted to the British Isles, except for some artificial introductions on the European continent.

The accentor family consists of a dozen species which are rather sparrow-like in general size and appearance. They are a widely distributed Palaearctic group, and only occur outside the region in south-western Arabia and on Formosa. Included in the family is the Dunnock or Hedge Sparrow (*Prunella modularis*), which is a familiar bird of the hedgerows, roadsides and gardens of Britain. The name Hedge Sparrow is a misnomer for it is, in fact, unrelated to the true sparrows. Another species that occurs in Europe is the Alpine Accentor (*Prunella collaris*). Most of the family live at high altitudes, and one species, the Himalayan Accentor (*Prunella himalayana*), breeds as high as 17,000 feet above sea-level.

Of the fifty-nine or sixty wrens, all but one are confined to the New World. The odd one out is the species which is found in Britain, which is simply called the Wren (*Troglodytes troglodytes*). This species, which is known in North America as the Winter Wren, is widely distributed throughout the Northern Hemisphere. The House Wren (*Troglodytes aedon*) is one of several other species which are found in North America.

Several hummingbirds occur in North America, the Rufous Hummingbird (*Selasphorus rufus*), even breeds as far north as south-eastern Alaska. Both the Calliope Hummingbird (*Stellula calliope*) and the Ruby-throated Hummingbird (*Archilochus colubris*) reach as far north as Canada. All three winter in Mexico. The Calliope Hummingbird, which is seldom found far from high mountains, is the smallest North American bird.

left
The tiny Wren, or Winter Wren
as it is called in America, is the
only member of this principally
New World family to have found its way
to Eurasia and North America

A female Red Grouse with her brood;
she incubates the eggs and rears the chicks
without any assistance from the male

Bills
and
Beaks

Birds' bills or beaks are one of several specialized features that distinguish them from other animals. They have many important functions, for not only are they used for feeding, but also for preening, nest building and sometimes as a weapon for attack or defence. The words 'bill' and 'beak' are generally regarded as being synonymous, although the term 'beak' is sometimes considered to include the jaws. The upper portion of the bill is known as the upper mandible and the lower portion as the lower mandible.

Most birds' bills are adapted to their feeding habits. The food factor has the greatest influence upon their shape and size, and there are innumerable adaptations for every kind of food and mode of feeding. Bills may be straight or may curve up or down or even sideways; some are very long, others very short. Crossbills have the ends of the two mandibles crossed over in a unique specialization for removing seeds from fir cones. Bills may be sharp and long, as in the herons and kingfishers which use them for spearing fish, or may be strong and broad, like those of finches and grosbeaks which use them for crushing large seeds or fruit kernels. The broad flat bills of swallows and flycatchers enlarge the effective area of the mouth so that insects can be scooped up while in flight. Some bills used for probing soft earth, like those of kiwis, woodcock and snipe, have sensitive tips.

Flamingos, invariably associated with brackish or salt-water lakes or lagoons, obtain their food from the water and mud, using the bill held upside down. Flamingos' bills are remarkable; they have internal fringes called lamellae which act as a filter, holding back the minute plant life and small water creatures upon which flamingos feed, while allowing the mud and water to escape. The Rosy Flamingo (*Phoenicopterus ruber*) has what is termed a shallow keeled bill in which small parts of the interior of the bill are covered with lamellae, while other flamingos have the inner surfaces of both mandibles entirely covered; this is known as a deep keeled bill. The diet of the flamingos with shallow keeled bills is more varied than that of the other species, and includes not only algae and diatoms upon which the others feed, but also small molluscs, crustaceans and the organic particles in mud. The difference in feeding habits probably accounts for the ability of the Greater (*Phoenicopterus ruber roseus*) and Lesser Flamingo (*Phoeniconaias minor*) to live side by side in such great numbers on the Rift Valley lakes in East Africa.

Another bird with a strange bill which sometimes lives alongside the flamingos on East African lakes is the African Spoonbill (*Platalea alba*). A bird of unmistakable appearance, it is one of a small group which have bills looking like large flattened wooden spoons. Spoonbills feed on aquatic crustaceans, molluscs, insects, and small fish. They feed while wading in shallow water, the bill being held almost vertically and partly open while it is moved rapidly from side to side. There are five species in the Old World, and just one, the Roseate Spoonbill (*Ajaia ajaja*), in the New World. Of similar size and build to the spoonbills are two species of open-billed storks (*Anastomus lamelligerus*) and (*Anastomus oscitanus*);

A Spoonbill feeding in a typical fashion in shallow water

The New Zealand Wrybill returning to its two eggs. This small plover uses its unique bill, which curves to the right, for probing for food under stones.

31

The enormous bulging bill of the Shoebill
or Whale-headed Stork may be adapted
for probing for lungfish
and other aquatic life
on the muddy bottoms of African swamps

Seen here in its breeding plumage,
the Turnstone uses its short stout bill
to lever up stones in search of food

one inhabits Africa and Malagasy, and the other
southern Asia. The bills of these two species of storks
have a large gap close to the tip which is probably an
adaptation for holding large slippery water-snails.

The most curious of all bills belongs to the Wrybill
(*Anarhynchus frontalis*) of New Zealand. This small
plover has a bill which curves sideways to the right.
It is a unique adaptation for seeking food under
stones. The Turnstone (*Arenaria interpres*) also
searches for food under stones, but instead has a
short stout bill which it uses for levering up and
overturning the stones. Another wading bird, the
avocet, has a long, thin, upcurved bill which it uses to
sweep the water in a side to side action with the
mandibles partly open.

Related to the gulls and terns, the skimmers,
sometimes called scissor-bills, have unique bills in
which the lower mandible is markedly longer than
the upper. They feed by flying close to the surface of
inland and coastal waters with the lower portion of
the bill just ploughing the water. When this strikes a
small fish or other aquatic animal, the upper
mandible clamps down on it in a scissor-like
movement, and it is then swallowed. When the
skimmer is newly hatched both mandibles are of
equal length, but as soon as the young bird begins to
develop feathers the more typical bill starts to become
evident.

In other species where the adult birds have
curiously shaped bills, such as the avocets, curlews
and flamingos, the young possess comparatively short
straight bills, which only slowly develop into the
more specialized bills of the adults. With most
species, however, the bills of the chicks closely
resemble those of their parents.

A widespread characteristic of the mouths of many
nestling birds, particularly those that are hatched
helpless, is that they are brightly coloured, often with
a number of contrasting spots on the tongue and
palate. These probably act as an aid or an inducement
to the parents to feed their gaping young. In the
embryo stage, birds develop a calcareous
protuberance on the tip of the upper mandible, known
as an 'egg tooth', the function of which is to aid the
chick to break its way out of the eggshell; it is shed
soon after hatching. Some species also have another
'egg tooth' on the lower mandible. In the case of
honeyguides which, like the cuckoo, lay their eggs in
other birds' nests, the young in addition possess a
sharp hook on the tip of each mandible which is shed
about the time the eyes open; with these hooks the
young parasites kill the nestlings of their host species.

Finches and grosbeaks and close allies such as the
buntings, weavers and sparrows which feed
principally on seeds, have short stout bills well
suited to their mode of feeding. They use their strong
bills to remove the outer shells from seeds in order to
obtain the kernel. The bill of the Hawfinch
(*Coccothraustes coccothraustes*), which is ridged on the
inside of the lower mandible, is able to crack the
stones of cherries and even olives. It has a crushing
power of as much as 150 pounds which, considering
that the bird only weighs about fifty-five grammes, is
remarkable. In North America, the Evening Grosbeak
(*Hesperiphona vespertina*) is sometimes called the
American Hawfinch on account of its large bill. The

An American Avocet showing its long thin
curved bill which it uses
in a side-to-side sweeping action to find
the aquatic life upon which it feeds

left
An Indian Skimmer with its clutch of eggs,
photographed in Delhi, India. The lower
mandible of the skimmer, which is larger
than the upper mandible, ploughs
the surface of the water as the bird flies
across it, and if it strikes a small fish
the mandibles are quickly closed and
the fish swallowed.

smallest of all seed-eating birds are the tiny waxbills, so named because some, like the Zebra Waxbill (*Estrilda subflava*) and Common Waxbill (*Estrilda astrild*), have red bills which look as though they are made of sealing wax.

The powerfully hooked and sharply pointed beaks which they use for killing and tearing up their food make birds of prey instantly recognizable. The Golden Eagle (*Aquila chrysaetos*) has a typical, strong tearing beak. Having killed its prey, the Golden Eagle firmly plants its feet on its victim, making maximum use of especially powerful inner claws, and proceeds to tear off pieces of flesh. Falcons have a tooth-like incision in their upper mandible that fits into a notch in the lower mandible and can be used to sever the bones of the neck of its victim. They are among the most accomplished fliers of all birds, and usually kill their prey, chiefly other birds, in full flight, either striking them dead with a blow from the hind claw or seizing them with their feet and bringing them to the ground. Other birds of prey have differently built beaks, suited to dealing with their particular type of prey. For example, some species such as the Lesser Kestrel (*Falco naumanni*) and cuckoo falcons or bazas (*Aviceda* spp.) feed principally on insects, and as a consequence have rather small and not especially strong beaks. A most unusual feature of the latter group is the presence of two serrations in the upper mandible which assist them to hold and dismember large insects.

Vultures' bills exhibit a wide variety of sizes and shapes. Some vultures have huge bills capable of tearing open carcasses, while others have smaller bills, ideal for feeding upon small pieces of flesh overlooked by the larger species. In Africa, one of the smaller species, the Egyptian Vulture (*Neophron percnopterus*), has a remarkable habit; picking up stones in its beak, it forcefully throws them at unguarded Ostrich eggs so as to break the shell and obtain the tasty contents. If there are no suitable stones close to the egg it has found, the Egyptian Vulture may search the surrounding ground for distances of up to fifty yards. One vulture is recorded as having managed to lift and throw a stone weighing over two pounds, an extraordinary feat for such a slender-billed bird measuring only twenty-one to twenty-six inches in length. It usually takes a vulture fewer than twelve direct hits to break the shell.

In contrast to the diurnal birds of prey, the owls have rather small, unexceptional beaks, similar in shape to one another. As much of their prey is swallowed whole, none has developed a very large bill for tearing flesh.

Another group of birds characterized by having strongly hooked bills are, of course, the parrots. Parrots' bills, however, are not designed for tearing flesh, but mainly for removing husks or the outer shells from seeds or nuts to feed on the contents; parrots are chiefly vegetarian, although some occasionally eat insects. They are very fond of most fruits and berries, and some species feed on nectar. Some, like the macaws, have heavy bills and fleshy tongues, and are capable of feeding on nuts which have extremely tough shells. The lories and lorikeets, which feed principally on pollen and nectar from flowers and also relish fruits and buds, have

relatively small bills and their tongues have a brush-like tip. When feeding, parrots often grasp their food in one foot and raise it to the bill to eat it. They will sometimes use their hooked bill as a third foot, to pull themselves along branches or up tree trunks.

Hummingbirds and sunbirds are among the birds which have elongated bills for probing flowers to obtain nectar. The majority of the New World's 300 or more species of hummingbirds have long, straight, thin bills, though some have down-curved bills, and a few have them curved upwards. The bill of the Sword-billed Hummingbird (*Ensifera ensifera*) is as long as the combined length of its head and body. Hummingbirds obtain their food, which not only includes nectar but also small insects, by hovering in

A Hawfinch using its enormous bill
to tackle a cherry

The Curlew, a common bird in the British Isles, uses its bill for probing marshy ground for the small animal life upon which it feeds

below
The head of a Secretary Bird showing the typical bill of a bird of prey

right
One of the world's smallest kingfishers,
the Pygmy Kingfisher measures no more
than 4 ins in length and feeds mainly on
small insects

left
Two Egyptian Vultures trying
to break open Ostrich eggs
in East Africa by dropping stones on them

above
The Kea of New Zealand which is reputed
to kill sheep by tearing away the wool
to feed on the fat and flesh

left
White-backed and Ruppell's Vultures
with a solitary Marabou Stork
at the carcass of a zebra

A Grey Parrot carefully holding a morsel of food in its foot as it nibbles at it

A Stripe-breasted Starthroat Hummingbird probing its long thin bill into a flower to feed on the nectar

A Malachite Sunbird perches on a protea bloom

front of flowers and probing their bill into them. While hovering, their wings may beat as many as fifty or more times per second, and be a mere blur to the human eye. Sunbirds usually feed from a perch, although they will sometimes hover. An Old World family unrelated to the hummingbirds, they all have long thin bills which curve downwards to varying degrees.

Woodpeckers are equipped with sturdy chisel-like bills for drilling for wood-boring insects and excavating nesting holes. The typical woodpeckers' bill is ideal for chiselling into wood, and is supported by a large head with a strong skull able to absorb shock. Woodpeckers also have extraordinarily long tongues, which in most species can be extended to astonishing lengths beyond the bill. The tongue is bordered with barbs at the tip, and when coated with a mucus from well-developed glands at its base, can be used for gathering up insects or licking sap from trees.

Seasonal ornamentation or appendages to the bill occur in some species. The American White Pelican (*Pelecanus erythrorhynchos*), for example, grows erect horny plates along the top of the upper mandible, which it loses after the breeding season. With puffins the much enlarged and laterally flattened and gaily decorated outer sheaths of the bill are shed after breeding, leaving smaller, unembellished bills of a different shape during the winter. The Puffin (*Fratercula arctica*) and the Horned Puffin (*Fratercula corniculata*) in addition to the plates on the bill, have coloured growths above and below the eye and fleshy rosettes at the gape. The male Knob-billed Goose or Comb Duck (*Sarkidiornis melanotos*) develops a remarkable, huge black comb on the upper mandible during the breeding season which, once breeding is finished, becomes less prominent. The bright red knob on the bill of the male Common Shelduck (*Tadorna tadorna*) also becomes less prominent outside the breeding season.

Two species from the Neotropical region have particularly weird appendages attached to their bills. These appendages, however, are permanent and are not shed. The Three-wattled Bellbird (*Procnias tricarunculata*) has a long thin fleshy wattle on top of the bill and another hanging on either side; the Mossy-throated Bellbird (*Procnias averane*) has a mass of fine fleshy wattles hanging like a beard from the throat. The reasons for this adornment are unknown.

Embellishments to the bill are seen in an extreme form in a number of the Old World hornbills. Many are made to look absurd by the addition of a cumbersome-looking growth on the top of the upper mandible known as a casque. Casques are permanent and may be of various shapes and sizes, and are usually smaller and less prominent in the females. One species which has an upturned casque is known as the Rhinoceros Hornbill (*Buceros rhinoceros*). Although the casque may make the bill appear too heavy for the bird to support, it is actually very light and usually made of a sponge-like cellular bony tissue. An exception is the casque of the Helmeted Hornbill (*Rhinoplax vigil*) which is solid and in consistency similar to ivory. In ancient times, such casques were prized imports into China where none but the finest craftsmen were allowed to carve

The Yellow-bellied Sapsucker,
an American species of woodpecker,
drills rows of holes
in lime trees and returns to
feed on the sap and small insects

A Great Spotted Woodpecker at its nesting
hole. Its extraordinarily long tongue
can be seen going into a hole in the trunk.

them. Only this species of hornbill, now found mainly in Borneo where it is confined to virgin forests in hilly country, has a sufficiently large and solid casque for this purpose.

Just why hornbills have such large bills surmounted by a casque is a mystery, but it has been suggested that it may have something to do with their unique nesting habits. All but the ground hornbills select a hole in a tree in which to nest, sealing the entrance with dung and other materials. During incubation the female is imprisoned in the nesting hole, with only a small gap through which the male can feed her. It is possible that the casque may be used as a trowel for walling up the nesting hole. Hornbills feed on fruits, berries, various insects and small animals. In order to transfer a morsel of food from the tip of its bill to its throat, a hornbill must toss it into the air with a backwards jerk of the head, then catch and swallow it. Toucans feed in a similar fashion.

Like hornbills, toucans have huge bills, but lack casques; instead, their bills are usually far more brightly coloured. The function of their gaily coloured bills is every bit as much a mystery as that of the hornbills. The largest toucan, the Toco Toucan (*Tucanus toco*) has an orange bill patterned with red, and a big black mark at the tip; another has a green bill with red, blue and orange markings. The bill of Swainson's Toucan (*Tucanus swainsoni*) is diagonally marked red and yellow. One suggestion is that because of their size and weight toucans must perch on the thick inner limbs of trees, and the bill may be an aid to them in reaching fruits growing on the thin outer branches.

This would explain the length, but not the bill's exceptional shape or its bright colours. Possibly the patterns and colours of the bill may serve as recognition marks between species with similarly coloured plumage. Another idea is that the brightly coloured bills may play some part in courtship displays, but this would seem unlikely as both male and female have equally gaily coloured bills. A further theory is that the long bill may help an incubating toucan to drive off enemies from the nesting hole; but most toucans will flee at the first sign of danger. As well as long bills, toucans have exceptionally long tongues; thin and horizontally flattened, they may reach a length of six inches in some of the larger species.

The difference in appearance between the male and female members of a species is called sexual dimorphism. Notable dimorphism in bill shape and size is uncommon, but was well illustrated in the bill of the Huia (*Heteralocha acutirostris*), a New Zealand bird which is thought to have become extinct in 1907. The male's bill was relatively short, stout, and almost straight, and the female's slender, down-curved and nearly twice as long as that of its mate. A pair sometimes co-operated in obtaining food from decayed wood; the male chiselled with his bill, while the female's long curved bill was used for probing. Differences in bills can also be seen in certain of the hornbills, some of which show considerable disparities in size and shape, as well as colour. The bills of male toucans tend to be slightly bigger than those of the females.

A male American Goldfinch using his
strong bill to crack sunflower seeds

Two Rosy Flamingos and a Greater
Flamingo feeding; they use their
highly specialized bills as filters

A Black and White-casqued Hornbill
showing the typical casque
on the upper mandible

The male Muscovy Duck, a familiar
farmyard creature, has a knob of bare red
skin at the base of its upper mandible

A Puffin showing the colourful
outer sheath to the bill which it assumes
in breeding dress

below
Unlike the American White Pelican which
grows erect horny plates along the top
of its bill during the breeding season,
the Dalmatian Pelican shown here grows
long feathers on its head

The Crested Serpent Eagle from
South East Asia kills snakes with
its typical bird of prey bill

right
A Hedge Sparrow feeding its young;
the brilliant scarlet lining of the
nestlings' mouths can be clearly seen

Few birds have such a large
and gaily coloured bill as the
Sulphur-breasted Toucan of Central
and northern South America

Behaviour

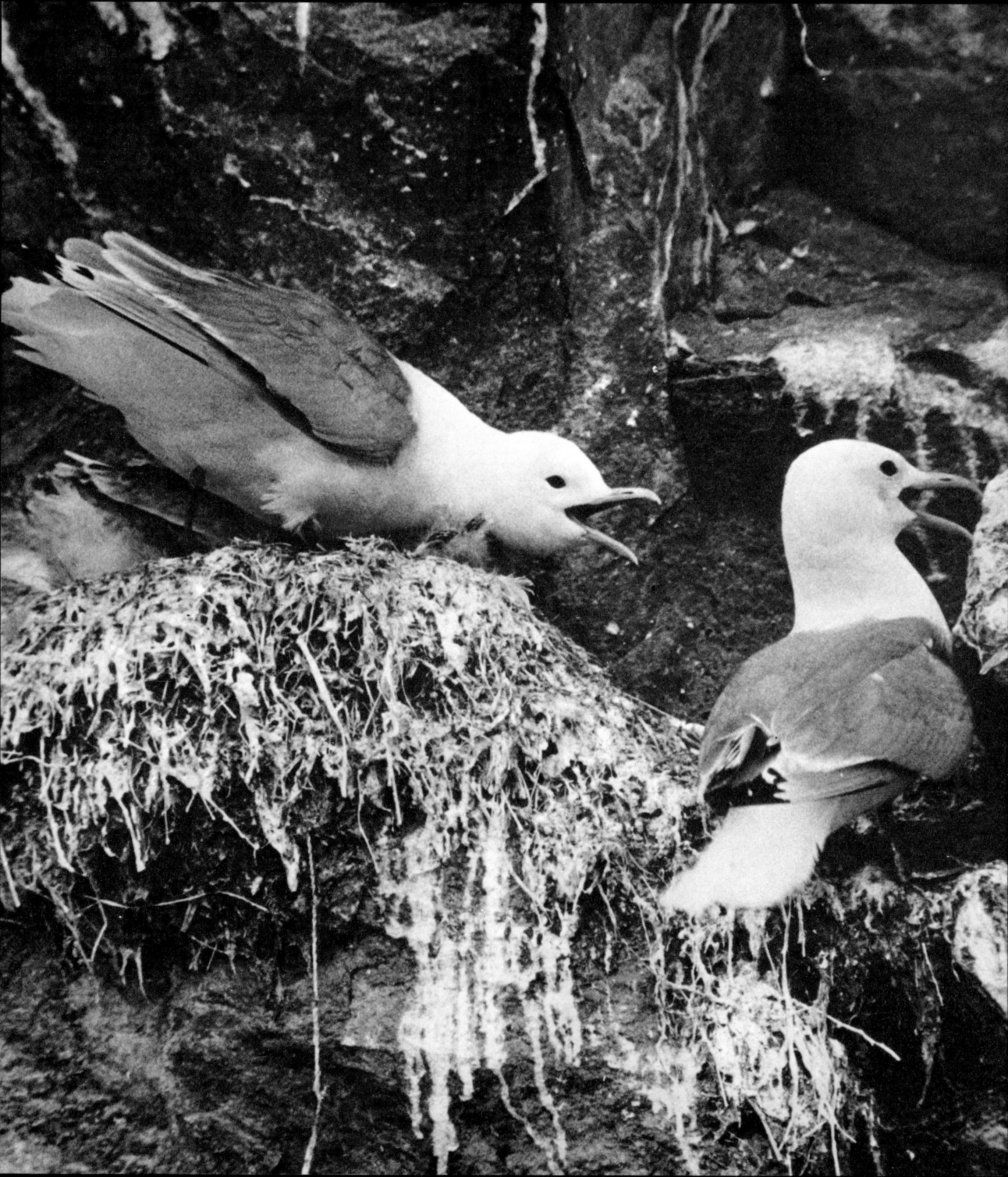

A bird's territory is an area which is defended primarily or exclusively against competing members of the same species. Such an area may be reserved by an individual, a pair, or a group. Birds are not unique in establishing territories; many other animals also have them. A territory may be defended in the breeding season only, for part of it, in the non-breeding season, or even the whole year round. It can vary enormously in size, and may be just an acre or two in extent for a small song bird, while for a large bird such as an eagle it may cover several square miles. The size of individual territories of the same species can vary considerably. In addition to this individual variation, there is often a strong tendency for territories to be smaller where food is more abundant. With some species it has also been noted that territories may be smaller when the population is larger than normal. The establishment of territories by birds results in the population of each species becoming spaced out, and is a highly efficient method of ensuring that a food supply is neither wasted nor exhausted. Spacing out promotes the use of empty habitats and tends to prevent overcrowding, with its resultant depletion of vital resources.

Although the defence of territory by birds was observed by Aristotle in the fourth century B.C., it was not until early in the present century that H. Eliot Howard demonstrated that territory plays an important part in bird behaviour, particularly in the breeding season. When they are breeding, most birds are confined to the neighbourhood of their nest, from which territory they exclude all intruders of the same species. A White Stork (*Ciconia ciconia*), for example, will permit sparrows to build in its nest and will not attack a man, but will repel other storks from the vicinity. Even in highly gregarious species which nest in huge colonies and build their nests in close proximity, each pair has its own jealously guarded territory, even if it is only a bill's length from its neighbour.

Among many small song birds, the territory probably safeguards a feeding area in which a pair has the sole rights to forage for food while rearing a family. This is likely to be of great importance to the survival of the young. The territory also provides a refuge for courting and mating, for it has been observed that when some species attempt to mate outside their territory, they are prevented from doing so by others of their own kind. The territory of a male Rook (*Corvus frugilegus*) is confined to its own nest and when mating within its own territory it is not molested, but outside its territory it is subjected to a hard buffeting. Many species, however, including most finches, use their nesting areas for courtship and rearing their broods, but forage over a wide space and do not have exclusive feeding territories.

Among birds that nest on the ground in colonies, such as terns and some gulls, one effect of having individual territories is to spread the nests in such a way as to minimize the risks of molestation by predators. For example, research has shown that this is very true of Black-headed Gulls (*Larus ridibundus*) which tend to space their nests one yard apart. If the nests are closer together crows can find the eggs more quickly, while if they are further apart it is likely that the concerted mobbing of predators becomes less

The aggressive wing flicking
of a Willow Warbler

The territory of many birds which nest
in colonies may be no more than
the distance they can reach from the nest
with their bill. Here a Kittiwake
threatens another which has come
too close to its nest.

effective, for the members of each pair only mob when a predator is almost or actually infringing their own territory. By nesting in close proximity penguins also get some measure of protection from egg stealers such as skuas and sheathbills. Some penguins will often violate the territory of others and steal stones from their neighbours' nests almost with impunity.

To divert the attention of predators from their eggs or nestlings, some species perform distraction displays. They may flutter or hobble about in an awkward manner as if injured, and will maintain the performance until they have led the enemy far from their eggs or young. The Ringed Plover (*Charadrius hiaticula*) and the Killdeer (*Charadrius vociferus*) are both adept at feigning injury if danger threatens, often dragging a wing as though it were broken. A female Mallard (*Anas platyrhynchos*) will sometimes flounder across a pool or lake to lead a predator away from her brood. The Purple Sandpiper (*Calidris maritima*) will imitate a small rodent to lead the Arctic Fox from its eggs or young. The fox which lives in the far north, where the sandpiper

A Rook driving an interloper
from its nesting territory

breeds, feeds chiefly on small rodents.

The friendly Robin, which is so familiar in many English gardens, is one of the most territorially minded of all birds. It is very unusual to encounter two adults in the same garden. During the spring the males use their powers of song to proclaim the ownership of a territory, and the red breast is used not, as might be imagined, in courtship, but as a threat display to rivals. After they have bred, both male and female claim a territory, and will even fight furiously for possession of it. The average size of a Robin's territory is one and a half acres.

David Lack, in his experiments with Robins, has demonstrated that even a bunch of red feathers placed in a Robin's territory will be savagely attacked. He began his experiments by setting up a stuffed Robin on the territory of an established bird, and found that the rightful owner approached, threatened, and finally attacked it. Once, the stuffed specimen was attacked so violently that its head was knocked off, yet the territory holder still continued its attacks. On discovering that the owner of the territory would even attack a headless bird, Lack removed further parts of the stuffed specimen, until only a bunch of red feathers from the Robin's breast remained, perched on a twig with a piece of wire for feet. He found it was just as effective as a complete bird in stimulating aggressive behaviour from the Robin. When an undamaged Robin with its breast painted brown was set up, the territory owner made no response.

Howard showed that song, which was previously thought to be used chiefly in courtship, is used mainly to announce ownership of a territory. A male bird normally sings only in its own territory, and the easiest means of mapping the territories of birds is to note where each is singing. The song announces occupation of the territory both to rival males and to females in search of a mate. Apart from singing, birds advertise their territorial rights in many different ways. Common Snipe (*Capella gallinago*) fly to a considerable height above their territory and then plunge earthwards in a fast fluttering dive, producing a drumming with their tail feathers. Both the Wood Pigeon (*Columba palumbus*) and Skylark (*Alauda arvensis*) also perform spectacular flights. Some hummingbirds fly in flights so curved that they appear to be tied to a central point by an invisible thread. During these flights their brilliantly coloured metallic throat gorgets flash a warning to likely rivals.

The nesting territory of birds of prey may vary in size between a few square yards of a cliff face as, for example, among some vultures which nest in colonies, to a large expanse of country for some eagles. Generally the nesting territory is defended against birds of the same species, but sometimes even birds of other species are driven away. Nests of such species as the Harpy Eagle (*Harpia harpyja*) of South America and the Crowned Eagle (*Stephanoaetus coronatus*) of Africa are seldom less than ten miles apart.

The study of the territory of birds—its survival value, and the way in which it is organized—is still very much in its infancy. A great deal of research is needed before it will be more fully understood.

A female Ostrich ruffles out her feathers
to make herself appear even larger as she
threatens an intruder near her nest

In order to frighten an enemy from
its nest and eggs an Avocet performs
an aggressive display, showing its bold
black and white markings

The fierce Great Skua will boldly
attack all intruders to its
breeding haunts, including humans

Gannets nesting on the island
of Grassholm off the coast of Wales.
Each bird's nest is about a bill's length
from that of its neighbour.

A pair of Nightingales attack the head
of a stuffed Cuckoo placed in their
territory; the parasitic Cuckoo lays its
eggs in the nests of other birds

A Robin standing guard
over its territory in autumn

below
A Dotterel acting as though
it were injured to distract
an enemy's attention from the nest

bottom
The threat display of
a female Superb Lyrebird

The friendly Robin of the English garden
is a highly aggressive bird, and will
savagely attack all other Robins
intruding into its territory, even
a stuffed specimen as in this picture

left
A Mute Swan vigorously attacks
an intruder into its territory.
Nesting Mute Swans are
extremely aggressive in defence of
their nest and young,
and will even attack human beings.

Bird
Calls
and Song

The sounds that birds make can be divided into two main categories: call-notes and true song. Call-notes can popularly be described as the language in which birds carry on their everyday conversations. They are concerned with the co-ordination of the behaviour of the other members of the same species, in such activities as feeding, flocking, migration and response to predators. Usually they tend to be short and simple. Not only must a bird be able to produce the correct call, but it must also have the innate ability to make the appropriate response to those of others, especially where the sound is giving warning of some immediate danger.

It is not, in fact, possible to draw a hard and fast line between call-notes and true song. Many examples of song can be found which appear to be little more than a series of call-notes. Call-notes, however, do seem to be inborn and instinctive, whereas songs usually have to be learnt.

Songs are part of a complex communication system that chiefly comes into operation during the breeding season. Usually they are performed by the male to proclaim a territory and defend it against possible intruders. By singing a territory holder may be saying that he is unmated, or may be broadcasting a message to likely rivals to tell them to keep away. Such a message will often act as a substitute for physical combat. Each species has its own special song for attracting a mate which differs from all other closely related birds. Sometimes the song is most important in preventing species which are very similar in appearance from pairing up and interbreeding.

It is very unusual for female birds to sing, particularly where there is a striking difference in plumage between the sexes. However, studies with ringed birds in recent years have shown that with some species it is not as rare as was formerly supposed. Elaborate songs have been heard from the male and female of a number of species; for example, it is known that the female Robin (*Erithacus rubecula*) will sing in the autumn when both sexes establish territories.

Many experiments have been conducted in order to discover more about song learning by birds. In this connection the song of the Chaffinch (*Fringilla coelebs*) has been studied more closely than any other species. Experiments with this species show that young Chaffinches learn some parts of their song from their male parent or other adults during the first two weeks of their life; most of the finer details of the song are acquired by the young bird when, in its first breeding season, it sings in competition with neighbouring territory holders. The young birds learn the song of the adults with whom they are in contact and preserve their geographical variations and dialects. Apart from a few exceptions, Chaffinches have been found to learn song patterns only during the first thirteen months of their life.

What has been learnt from the experiments with Chaffinches cannot, of course, be applied to all other birds. One species, the White-crowned Sparrow (*Zonotrichia leucophrys*), has been discovered to learn its song during the first 100 days of its life, when it cannot sing, storing up the information to use later. The precise effect of this kind of

The weird cries of the Laughing Kingfisher or Kookaburra have earned it many popular names in Australia, including Laughing Jackass and Settler's Clock

The Nightingale is thought by many to be the finest of all bird singers; despite its name it also sings during the day

57

It is known that both the male
and female Robin will sing
to proclaim their territories

experience probably varies from species to species.
It is likely that species such as the Cuckoo
(*Cuculus canorus*), which are not reared by their own
kind, are able to develop their full vocal repertoire
without learning from adults of their own species.

Learning to recognize the individual sounds of
other members of the same species can be
particularly important in the rearing of young and in
the maintenance of a family bond. This is likely to
apply very much to species that nest in colonies
where there are a large number of chicks of about the
same age, size and appearance. It seems likely that it
is by sounds that each parent is able to pick out its
own offspring in such colonies. Flamingos
probably use this means, and so do penguins.

During the weeks after its chick hatches, the
parent King Penguin (*Aptenodytes patagonica*)
spends long periods murmuring to it. During this
period of indoctrination the chick learns to
recognize the individual sound of the adult by its
apparently characteristic rhythm. Later, the chicks
form into huge groups, sometimes called crèches,
which may contain many hundreds or even
thousands of birds, while the parents go off in search
of food for them. When the parents return from the
sea with food, they stand around the edge of the
milling mass of youngsters and call out persistently
until the youngsters recognize their individual
parents' calls and come out of the group to be fed.

The manner in which birds produce their calls and
songs is entirely different from that of other living
creatures, including man. Whereas human beings
use the upper larynx, birds make their sounds by
means of the syrinx. Birds have a larynx, but it has
no vocal cords and has little or no part in voice
production. The syrinx is usually located at the point
where the windpipe divides into two tubes leading
into the lungs. Among various groups of birds the
syrinx varies enormously in shape, complexity, and
even in position. Although it is not usually possible
to find a direct link between the shape of the syrinx
and the type of sound produced, it has been
discovered that those birds with the most
complicated type of syrinx have the best and most
varied songs.

No other bird in the world has inspired so much
poetry and romance as the Nightingale (*Luscinia
megarhynchos*), thanks to the beauty of its song
which many people consider unrivalled. The fact that
the Nightingale frequently sings during the hours of
darkness when most other birds are silent is no
doubt responsible for much of the hold it has on the
imagination of the public. It sings just as often by
day, but then the song mingles with those of other
birds and loses much of its individuality. An
unimpressive-looking bird, it is plain brown on the
upperparts and lighter below, rather like a large
brown Robin. The song, which seems much too
vigorous and loud to come from so small a bird, is
usually delivered from the cover of a low tree.

Another fine songster is the Shama (*Copsychus
malabaricus*), a species which inhabits the forests of
South East Asia. It is a bird which is constantly in
demand as a cage-bird on account of its fine song.
Some consider that at its best the song of the male
Shama is superior to that of the Nightingale. The

The Canary, which is a native of
the Azores, Madeira and
the Canary Islands, was first domesticated
in Britain as a cage-bird towards the end
of the sixteenth century

below
A male Chaffinch at its nest.
Young Chaffinches only learn
song patterns during the first
13 months of their life.

The Mute Swan is not completely silent
as its name suggests;
its wings also produce a strange,
beating sound in flight

top
A male Superb Lyrebird singing
on its territory in Sherbrooke Forest,
Victoria, Australia

above
The Common Starlings shown here belong
to a family which contains some of
the most accomplished of bird mimics

Few birds are better able to imitate
human speech than the Greater Hill Mynah

Shama is a small bird with a long tail, and like the
Nightingale belongs to the thrush family. Mainly
glossy black, the male has chestnut underparts and a
white rump and outer tail feathers. The 'Pekin
Robin' or Red-billed Leiothrix (*Leiothrix lutea*) is
another species very popular with aviculturists for
its song.

Of all cage-birds kept for their singing ability, the
best known is the Canary. The many domesticated
varieties we know today are descended from the wild
Canary (*Serinus canaria*), a finch native to the
Canary Islands, the Azores and Madeira. This bird
was domesticated in Britain towards the end of the
sixteenth century, having previously been introduced
into Italy in 1510 from the Canary Islands. The wild
Canary is olive-green with dark streaking above and
yellowish below. Originally an indifferent songster,
it has been bred selectively in confinement for
centuries; many varieties with fine songs have now
evolved.

Several groups of birds are known to be capable of
duetting, that is, two members of a pair singing
simultaneously as part of the courtship display or to
maintain the pair bond. The Black-headed Gonolek
(*Laniarius erythrogaster*) is one of a number of
species which have been observed in a very special
type of duetting known as antiphonal singing.
Different notes are sung by the male and female, and
the pair may alternate their parts with such
extraordinarily accurate timing that, unless one is
actually watching the performance, it may be
impossible to tell that the song is not the work of a
single bird. The speed of the response of one bird to
the other is far more accurate than that of which
human beings would be capable. Duetting reaches its
highest development in the African shrikes of the
genus to which the Black-headed Gonolek belongs,
and is also known among some barbets, grass
warblers and other species.

What the use of duetting is to the birds which
practise it is uncertain, but it may be a method of
mutual recognition and communication between the
two members of a pair in species inhabiting dense
vegetation. It appears to be more or less restricted to
species found in the tropics.

While many birds learn their songs, or at least
some parts of them, by imitating others of their own
kind, some species incorporate into their songs
sounds copied from other species or even from
objects or things other than birds. The tendency to
mimic is best found in such species as the Starling
(*Sturnus vulgaris*), the Marsh Warbler
(*Acrocephalus palustris*) and North American
Mockingbird (*Mimus polyglottos*). Mimicry has been
developed to an extraordinary degree by the lyrebirds
in Australia. Amongst their repertoire may be the
calls of many birds and mammals, as well as such
sounds as the whine of a circular saw, the hoot of a
car horn or whistle of a railway engine. Some of the
African robin-chats are also particularly fine mimics.
It is not known why birds use vocal mimicry, but it
is likely to serve a purpose similar to duetting.

Quite a number of species, when kept in captivity,
learn to imitate human speech. Although in
confinement these birds may sometimes imitate a
particular person or person's speech with outstanding

The Jackass Penguin is so called because of its braying call which is very like the braying of a donkey

accuracy, unlike human beings they do not understand the meanings of the sounds they make. Those species best able to imitate human speech include many members of the parrot family, and the hill mynahs of South East Asia. I have also known Splendid Glossy Starlings (*Lamprocolius splendidus*) able to imitate human speech, as well as a wide range of other man-made and mechanical sounds.

The species most commonly kept for its ability to 'talk' is the Budgerigar (*Melopsittacus undulatus*), a native of Australia. This tiny Australian parrakeet was first brought alive from Australia by Gould in 1840. In its natural environment its plumage is mainly green, but by selective breeding from mutations a great variety of colour forms have been evolved. Other members of the parrot family prized for their ability to talk include the amazon parrots of Central and South America and the Grey Parrot (*Psittacus erithacus*) of Africa.

Each year huge numbers of nestling hill mynahs known in the trade as 'gapers' are imported into Europe and the U.S.A. Here they become household pets, and in their new homes are hand-reared and later trained to speak. Few birds are able to imitate human speech better than a good Greater Hill Mynah (*Gracula religiosa intermedia*). Sometimes they will acquire a large vocabulary of words and phrases, and also learn to imitate other sounds, such as human coughs and laughs, with uncanny accuracy. The Greater Hill Mynah is a little smaller than a jackdaw, and its plumage is chiefly black, with a purple, blue and green sheen. It has a stout, orangey-yellow bill and legs, and fleshy yellow wattles on the head and neck. Birds kept on their own with plenty of human company usually learn to speak far better than those housed with other birds.

Some species produce very unusual sounds. For instance, the Naked-throated Bellbird (*Procnias nudicollis*) makes a dull resounding 'clonk', reminiscent of a metal object being struck. The Bell Miner (*Manorina melanophrys*) is said to produce a sound resembling the tinkling of a silver bell. The Jackass Penguin (*Spheniscus demersus*) is so called because of its braying call, which sounds very like the braying of a donkey. Likened to various sounds, including a distant foghorn and the far-off 'moo' of a

The bill clattering or greeting display of a pair of White Storks

cow, the curious 'boom' of the Bittern (*Botaurus stellaris*) is uttered during the spring. It has extraordinary carrying power and can be heard with ease over two miles away.

In India the Hawk Cuckoo (*Cuculus varius*) is also known as the Brain-fever Bird. It closely resembles a small hawk, the Shikra, in both adult and juvenile plumages, and the likeness extends to many of its habits. The Hawk Cuckoo is notorious for its irritatingly monotonous cry during the hottest weather. This call is repeated on an ascending scale, getting more and more excited, until it suddenly stops—only to start again at the bottom of the scale a few moments later. The cry suggests the words 'brain fever' and gives the bird its alternative name, or perhaps the maddening repetition of its call is thought to precipitate the disease! In Hindi it is said to be crying 'where is my love?'

Many kingfishers have loud calls, not least the renowned Laughing Kingfisher or Kookaburra (*Dacelo novaeguineae*) of Australia. This giant kingfisher has a weird cry that is often uttered in chorus with other Kookaburras; its human-sounding laughter and the regularity of its early morning call have given rise to such popular names as Laughing Jackass, Happy Jack and Settler's Clock. Another group of birds named for their calls are the trumpeters of South America; the Indians often take advantage of their loud and distinctive voices by keeping them with their poultry as 'watchdogs'. In North America this name is given to the huge Trumpeter Swan (*Cygnus cygnus buccinator*) because of its trumpeting or bugle-like call.

The Mute Swan (*Cygnus olor*), despite its name, is by no means a silent bird although it is less vocal than other swans. There are some birds, however, which appear to be practically voiceless. The best examples are the storks, for most are capable of no more than low grunts and hisses, although a few are able to produce one or two melodious notes. The main sound uttered by some storks is a loud clattering of the mandibles. White Storks (*Ciconia ciconia*) greet their mate by throwing back the head until it almost rests on the back, and clattering the bill like castanets. In addition to their normal calls, owls will clatter their bills loudly as a threatening gesture.

The ability to produce sounds by means other than the voice is by no means confined to some of the storks and owls. Many woodpeckers rapidly strike their bills against branches to produce a drumming sound; each species has its own recognizable tattoo, differing from others in duration, number of taps, and intensity of rhythm. During display flights the Common Snipe (*Capella gallinago*) rapidly dives from a considerable height and makes a drumming noise which is produced by the vibration of the specially modified outermost tail feathers, while Wood Pigeons (*Columba palumbus*) produce a vigorous clap with their wings. The Ruffed Grouse (*Bonasa umbellus*) of North America makes a rattle like a machine-gun by beating its wings against its breast. Some swans and ducks make a loud swirling sound with their wings when they take off from water and in the air, while the hummingbirds take their name from the humming noise produced by their wings while in normal flight.

A Bittern brooding its chicks.
The curious 'boom' uttered by the Bittern has extraordinary carrying power and may be heard over 2 miles away.

Courtship and Display

When a peacock raises his beautiful elongated feathers and brings them up over his head to form a gorgeous fan, he is displaying to attract a mate. The display performed by the peacock is just one of the many wonderful displays performed by birds. The long ornamental feathers which the peacock uses in display are not, as is often supposed, the tail feathers, but are elongated feathers coming from the base of the tail. Like the peacock, the males of many other species also possess special feathers which play a leading part in their displays. These feathers are often part of the tail or wings, and may be particularly distinctively patterned or brightly coloured, or perhaps especially elongated or strangely shaped. Sometimes they may also take the form of plumes, or other kinds of unusual feathering growing from various parts of the body. Some species, like the male frigatebirds, do not have brightly coloured or unusual plumage but instead possess a brilliantly coloured throat pouch which they are able to inflate to attract the attention of a likely mate. Male birds which perform the most elaborate displays often do so in the company of a number of others, and many that display on the ground clear special display areas.

As with most male birds that possess especially bright plumage and have elaborate displays, the peahens that the male peafowl tries to attract are very soberly coloured. The female Blue or Common Peafowl (*Pavo cristatus*), which is the species most commonly kept in zoos and on many country estates, is principally a dull blackish-brown, except for a lighter belly and a green sheen on the neck. In contrast, the peacock or male is a glossy blue with a barred back and has a splendid train of long green feathers, each tipped with an 'eye'.

The Blue Peafowl, of which white, pied, and black-shouldered mutations occur in captivity, is a native of India and Ceylon. A second species of peafowl, the Green Peafowl (*Pavo muticus*), differs from the Common Peafowl principally in being green and in having a more fully feathered crest; the female also has a brighter plumage.

As with the peafowl, most male pheasants are extremely gaily coloured and perform exciting displays. Perhaps the most spectacular is performed by the male Argus Pheasant (*Argusianus argus*). Unlike most other pheasants, the male Argus Pheasant is not brilliantly coloured, but instead is brown spotted and marked with chestnut, black, and buff. He has, however, the most extraordinary inner flight feathers, for they are greatly elongated, broadened, and adorned with a row of 'eyes'. During display, the wings are held open and flattened vertically, with the head hidden behind them, giving the appearance of a huge, beautifully decorated fan.

The development of special feathers to attract the attention of the opposite sex reaches its peak among many of the male birds of paradise. Not only do their feathers exhibit an enormous range of brilliant colours, but also an astonishing array of weird and fanciful shapes. The males with the most brightly coloured plumage generally have very dull-coloured mates. Where there is a great difference in appearance between the sexes, pairs are not usually formed; instead, the females visit the males' display places, mate, and then nest and raise their young

This back view of a displaying peacock clearly shows that it is not, as is often supposed, the tail feathers which are used in display, but long ornamental feathers coming from their base. The bird shown here is a white mutation of the Blue Peacock.

Watched by a female at the back of the bower, a male Greater Bowerbird displays with a bone in its bill

independently of the males. With some of the more soberly coloured species, both sexes look alike and share the nesting duties. Apart from their close relationship with the bowerbirds, the forty or so species of birds of paradise seem to be most akin to the crows. Their main stronghold is New Guinea and its islands, with a few species in northern Australia and the Molucca Islands.

One of the largest species is the Greater Bird of Paradise (*Paradisaea apoda*). The male of this species is chiefly rich brown, except for a yellow head with a brilliant green gorget, and long golden flank plumes. He begins his courtship by uttering loud, raucous cries, then starts to dance, usually along the branch of a tree. As the dance progresses, he leans forward, lowers his wings and throws the plumes up over his back. It is usual for a number of males to dance together. In the early 1900s when it was feared that this magnificent species might become extinct because so many were slaughtered for their plumes, a number were taken from the Aru Islands and introduced on to little Tobago in the West Indies. Descendants of these birds still live on this tiny Caribbean island.

Named after Austria's Crown Prince Rudolph, the Blue Bird of Paradise (*Paradisaea rudolphi*) has blue plumes. The male Blue Bird of Paradise, which has principally blue and black plumage, displays hanging upside down from a branch with its plumes falling on each side of its body. The King Bird of Paradise (*Cicinnurus regius*), which has a body length of not much more than six inches, is the smallest of the birds of paradise. The plumage of the male is mainly a shimmering red, with a pure white belly. In addition he has fan-like plumes tipped with emerald green, which normally lie hidden under the bend of the wing, and two sweeping tail wires, each tipped with a twist of gleaming green feather. When he displays he opens his wings and expands the fans which were previously hidden, bringing the tail wires up over his back. He raises his head obliquely upwards and constantly sways it slightly from side to side. He will also open his wings so that they are cupped, and vibrate them; sometimes the male will even do this hanging upside down, with the bill open so that the green gape is shown.

The male King of Saxony Bird of Paradise (*Pteridophora alberti*), with black and deep yellow plumage, is notable for his head plumes, which may be eighteen inches long, more than twice the length of the bird. He has two plumes, one coming from each side of the head just behind the eye. They are wire-like and have a series of small, celluloid-like 'flags' along one side. The male displays on a branch high in a tree, tossing the long head ornaments into the air above his head. The male Six-plumed Bird of Paradise (*Parotia sefilata*) has three wires tipped with a black racquet coming from each side of the head. During display, the male draws long, velvety-black, ornamental plumes around his body to form a skirt.

As part of their courtship, some birds like the Satin Bowerbird (*Ptilonorhynchus violaceus*) construct an avenue of twigs, called a bower. The Satin Bowerbird is a native of eastern Australia, about the size of a jackdaw. The male is almost entirely a glossy purplish-blue in colour, while the

The male Greater Bird of Paradise raises its beautiful golden flank plumes over its head during its display

right
The dark-coloured male Satin Bowerbird seems to be paying very little attention to a female which has come to visit his bower

left
A male Red-plumed Bird of Paradise
displaying. This species is one of
the largest members of the family.

above
A back view of a male Great Bustard
displaying. The tail is raised and
the wings held open so as to expose
a large expanse of white plumage
not normally seen.

left
A maypole builder, the male Golden
Bowerbird although only just over
9 ins in length may nevertheless
build a cone of twigs around a sapling
to a height of about 9 ft

female is mainly olive-green with the underparts barred. The bower, which may consist of thousands of small twigs stuck upright into a patch of clear ground, is the work of the male alone. He decorates his bower with blue objects and also paints it with masticated fruit-pulp using a wad of leaves or piece of bark as a paint-brush. Having attracted a female to the bower the male dances and shows off, often with objects from the bower held in his bill. The display may continue for several weeks until the forest becomes seasonally full of the insect life on which the young will be fed. It is only then that the female mates with the male. Afterwards she leaves the bower and goes off alone to build a nest and raise a family.

The dull-coloured male Gardener Bowerbird (*Amblyornis inornatus*) with plumage indistinguishable from the female's builds an extraordinary bower like a miniature native hut. This structure which may be three feet high is built around the base of a small sapling, and is surrounded by a carefully tended garden, decorated with flower petals and other objects, which are renewed almost daily. This species, which is known as a maypole builder, is smaller than the Satin Bowerbird and inhabits New Guinea.

Black Grouse (*Tetrao tetrix*) gather at display grounds known as 'leks' which are usually situated in a meadow or on open moorland. The appearance of the male, known as a Blackcock, is unmistakable. Almost his entire plumage including a lyre-shaped tail is black with a glossy blue sheen, except for white under-tail feathers and a bar on the wing. Above his eye there is a red wattle. The female, which also has a red wattle over the eye, is smaller than the male and is brown with blackish barring. She is known as a Greyhen, while both sexes are collectively called Blackgame. The Black Grouse inhabits a large area of the Palaearctic region.

The Blackcocks meet at the leks to display, particularly during spring and early summer. Such gatherings usually take place at dawn but may sometimes occur just before sunset. As many as twenty Blackcocks may assemble daily at the traditional leks where each bird has an individual territory often called a 'court'. Territorial boundaries are maintained by repeated confrontations between neighbouring birds, which threaten each other in ritual fashion but only rarely indulge in serious fighting. In their display Blackcocks strut about with their wings drooped and their tail erect and fanned, showing off the white under-tail feathers. The throat and chest are puffed out and the whole body is vibrated. There is much hissing and crowing, including a remarkable bubbling call, and often they make short flights into the air.

It is not until the males have been displaying for some time that the Greyhens start to make an appearance at these dawn gatherings. First one or two females visit the lek for short periods, then as the season advances their number increases and they stay longer. At first the females stay near the boundaries of the lek away from the males, which respond to the females' arrival with much excitement. As time progresses, the Greyhens become more interested and begin to walk through

A Blackcock displaying on a lek

A Wood Pigeon caressing its mate.
This and similar display acts help to bring the pair into full breeding condition.

A cock Sage Grouse spreading out its huge tail feathers as part of its display

the territories among the displaying males. They go from territory to territory, often in the company of a number of other females, and may be courted by most of the males at the lek. After about half a dozen visits the female is ready to mate. Research has revealed that one male may mate with most of the females that visit the lek, while some other males may not mate at all.

Once a female has mated it is unlikely that she will return to the lek again. Instead she will go off and search for a nesting site, where she will lay seven or eight eggs which will be hatched and reared without the aid of a mate. Meanwhile, the Blackcocks remain at the lek displaying to each other and still defending their territories. Other grouse which maintain leks are the Capercaillie (*Tetrao urogallus*), prairie chickens (*Tympanuchos cupido* and *Tympanuchos pallid icinctus*), Sharp-tailed Grouse (*Tympanuchos phasianellus*) and Sage Grouse (*Centrocercus urophasianus*); the latter four species are North American.

In breeding plumage the Ruff (*Philomachus pugnax*) has an extraordinary appearance, for its head is adorned with a wonderful 'Elizabethan' ruff and projecting ear tufts. The ruff and ear tufts vary enormously in colour and pattern from bird to bird: they may be black, various shades of brown and chestnut, and even buff or white. The Reeve, as the female is called, is smaller than the male and lacks his decorations. Outside the breeding season both

A cock Sage Grouse inflates the air-sacs on either side of its neck to enormous size in its efforts to attract a mate

sexes look alike. The arenas where Ruffs gather together to display are called 'hills' and are usually situated in grassy meadows. At the hills the males crouch facing each other, puffing out their ruffs and showing-off. They are unusual in that at their hills they are silent; in addition, every male at a display arena has a differently coloured ruff.

Other groups which have display grounds or leks are the manakins and cock-of-the-rocks. The manakins which inhabit forested regions of Central and South America are tiny birds, often extremely attractively coloured. Gould's Manakin (*Manacus vitellinus*) clears itself a small patch on the forest floor, taking away all the leaves and other debris that is small enough to be carried. The clear patch selected normally contains a vertical sapling on which the male dances and jumps about. He also produces loud snapping and whirring noises with specially modified wing feathers. The females visit the males at their display arenas and will sometimes join them in their dancing.

Two male Blue-backed Manakins (*Chiroxiphia pareola*) will regularly dance together side by side on a branch, jumping up and down alternately. When a female visits their display perch they will face her and jump up and down and show off to her. The male Blue-backed Manakin is almost entirely velvety-black, except for a deep red cap and a pale blue 'saddle' on its back; the female is uniformly olive-green. In contrast to the very active displays performed by the manakins, the much larger Cock-of-the-rock (*Rupicola rupicola*) adopts a static posture on the display arena which it may hold for several minutes.

In the undergrowth of its forest home, the male Superb Lyrebird (*Menura novaehollandiae*) may prepare as many as ten circular clearings as display arenas. Each clearing is about three feet in diameter and is slightly raised above the ground to form a mound on which the male may display several times a day. At the height of his performance he brings his wonderful tail feathers up over his head. In addition he prances about, singing not only his own notes but also imitating a wide variety of other birds.

Nearly all male birds which regularly display at arenas are equipped with striking adornments or, like Gould's Manakin, with means of producing unusual sounds; some have both. The sounds produced probably help females to locate them, especially those which dwell in forests. In spite of the danger from predators which may be attracted by their gay plumage and the fact that they regularly display at the same site, the males of most of these species are very successful in maintaining their numbers. The females, which undertake all the domestic duties, are far less conspicuous than the males, and in accordance with the general principles of adaptive coloration, tend to be cryptically coloured.

Instead of possessing brightly coloured or unusually shaped feathers to attract a mate, male frigatebirds have a bright red throat pouch which they inflate like a balloon. Largest of the five species is the Magnificent Frigatebird (*Fregata magnificens*), which ranges from the Galapagos Islands and the eastern Pacific to the Caribbean, the Cape Verde Islands, and the coast of West Africa. Except for his red throat pouch, the male Magnificent Frigatebird is all black

The ruffs and ear-tufts of Ruffs vary enormously in colour and pattern from bird to bird. These two displaying males were photographed near Amsterdam in Holland.

A Ruff pauses for a moment's rest in its display

With the tail brought forward and lowered completely over the head, the male Superb Lyrebird prances about and sings on one of its mounds in the forest undergrowth

Instead of brightly coloured feathers to attract a mate, the male Magnificent Frigatebird possesses a brilliant red throat pouch which he is able to inflate like a balloon

with a purple and green sheen. The female, which lacks a throat pouch, is on average slightly larger than the male. Her plumage is blackish-brown with a white chest.

Normally frigatebirds nest in colonies, chiefly on islands where there is little disturbance by man. The male takes up a nesting site in a tree or low bush and then sets about attracting females flying overhead. He inflates his throat pouch until it is about as large as a man's head, spreads his wings, ruffles his feathers out, and rattles his bill. When he has attracted a mate, they both start building a nest mainly of sticks, and together incubate the single white egg, which may may take forty to fifty days to hatch.

With some species the roles of the sexes are reversed. Female phalaropes, for example, are larger than the males and in breeding plumage are more richly coloured. The females are the first to arrive at the breeding grounds and also take the initiative in the courtship. The eggs are incubated exclusively by the male, although the female commonly remains at hand and may, at least in the case of the Grey Phalarope (*Phalaropus fulicarius*), share in tending the chicks. The Grey Phalarope is known as the Red Phalarope in North America because of its dark chestnut breeding plumage. There are two other species of these small sandpiper-like waders, the Red-necked or Northern Phalarope (*Phalaropus lobatus*) and Wilson's Phalarope (*Steganopus tricolor*). Wilson's Phalarope which breeds in North America and winters in the tropics and South America is essentially a fresh-water bird. The other two species, which are northern circumpolar breeders, spend the winter well out to sea in warmer waters.

The roles of the sexes are also reversed among the painted snipes. There are just two species; they show only a superficial resemblance to the true snipe and are not closely related to them. The smaller of the two species is the American Painted Snipe (*Nycticryphes semicollaris*) which is confined to South America, while the other occurs throughout most of the warmer regions of the Old World, and is known simply as the Painted Snipe (*Rostratula benghalensis*). The female of the latter species has a spectacular courtship display in which she spreads her wings and brings them forward beyond the tip of the bill, at the same time fanning her tail to reveal a number of bright spots. The male, which has a duller plumage than the female, undertakes all the domestic duties once the eggs have been laid. With the American Painted Snipe it is the female which incubates the two eggs.

Among the approximately fifteen species of buttonquail, also, the female is the larger, the more brightly coloured, and takes the leading part in courtship. Both sexes make the nest, but the male does most of the incubation and rears the young. It is likely that the female lays several clutches of eggs to be attended by different males. This may also be true of the female Painted Snipe, and it is suspected that this happens sometimes with phalaropes. The eggs of the tinamous, which are outstanding for their heavily polished appearance and beautiful vivid colours, are also incubated by the male alone. Similarly the male rhea incubates and he may tend the eggs of a number of females all laid in a single nest which he has made.

To attract a mate the Blue Peacock
brings its beautiful train of feathers
up over its back to form a gorgeous fan

During the breeding season the male Capercaillie, here seen displaying, becomes so aggressive that it will even attack humans

below
The male Spotted Bowerbird of eastern Australia uses shells to decorate the entrance to its bower

Unusual
Nests

Once a bird has courted and won a mate, it usually sets about choosing a nesting site and building a nest. Some species, of course, like guillemots and razorbills, make no attempt to build a nest, but lay their eggs on a bare rock, while some like the Old World cuckoos, lay their eggs in other birds' nests, to be hatched and reared by a host species. Others, like the pigeons and doves build a very flimsy structure. The great majority, however, build cup- or saucer-shaped nests. A few build very elaborate or unusual nests.

The most incredible nesting structure built by any bird is the huge communal dwelling constructed by the Social Weaver (*Philetairus socius*). It is built among the limbs of a tree, often a big acacia, preferably standing alone in the open. This structure, which is made from grasses and small thorny twigs, may consist of as many as 100 individual nests built close together and united under a single roof. All the occupants of a colony, both males and females, build and maintain the roof which is thatched in such a way that the rain runs off and does not soak through. Such a structure may measure thirty by twenty feet at the base and be five feet high. Before and after the breeding season the nests are used for roosting. Social Weavers are small birds, mainly brown and black, which live in southern Africa.

In southern Africa, the Pygmy Falcon (*Poliohierax semitorquatus*), the smallest African bird of prey, does not build a nest of its own, but uses that of a Social Weaver. The weavers do not object to the presence of the tiny falcon, which does not molest its hosts. In East Africa where the Social Weaver does not occur, the falcon nests in the abandoned homes of buffalo weavers. The two species of buffalo weavers, the Black (*Bubalornis albirostris*) and the White-headed (*Dinemellia dinemelli*), do not build communal structures but large untidy domed nests of thorny twigs as a protection against unwelcome visitors.

Some weavers add to their nests a long entrance tube, which hangs down vertically below the nesting chamber. The entrance tube, which may be two feet or more in length, helps to prevent predators such as snakes from entering the chamber and eating the eggs or young or perhaps even the incubating adult. One species which attaches an especially long entrance tube to its nest is the Baya Weaver (*Ploceus philippinus*) which inhabits parts of South East Asia.

Like the Social Weaver, the Quaker or Grey-breasted Parrakeet (*Myiopsitta monachus*) of South America nests in huge communal structures built of twigs, in which each pair has a separate chamber. Also like the weavers, when they are not breeding, the parrakeets use their nesting chambers as sleeping quarters. They continue to add more twigs to the structure year after year, until it becomes too heavy for the branches that support it, and they break. The Quaker Parrakeet is the only member of the parrot family to nest in this fashion.

Most woodpeckers excavate a hole in a tree to nest in, but the Buff-spotted Woodpecker (*Campethera nivosa*) bores a hole in a tree ants' nest and hollows out a cavity in which to lay its two white eggs. The ants do not seem to molest the woodpeckers, and the woodpeckers appear to refrain from eating their hosts. In the East African bush, the Red and Yellow Barbet (*Trachyphonus erythrocephalus*) will nest in

The communal dwelling of a colony of sparrow weavers

Two young Wood Thrushes begging for food. The nest of this North American thrush is very similar to that built by the British Song Thrush.

Brünnich's Guillemots make no nest but simply lay their single egg on a bare rocky ledge

A male Mallee Fowl filling in the centre of its nesting mound; the heat generated by rotting vegetation incubates the eggs

above
This pair of Blue-footed Boobies have
built no nest, but merely raised their
two chicks in a scrape in the ground

right
A young Greater Spotted Woodpecker,
almost big enough to leave
the nesting hole, being fed by its parent

left
Weavers' nests hanging from a tree in
Kenya, like some strange exotic fruit

below
The Stone Curlew makes no nest but
lays her two eggs, which match
their surroundings well, in an unlined
scrape in the ground

bottom left
A recently hatched Bronze Cuckoo caught
in the act of tipping one of
its hosts' eggs from the nest,
in this case Red-capped Robins

above
Perched on its flimsy nest of sticks,
a Wood Pigeon feeds its single chick

Part of a nesting colony of cormorants
on Lake Malawi, Africa; the large untidy
nests are lined with bits of vegetation
or a few feathers

A Great Crested Grebe on its nest
of floating vegetation; this species
occurs widely in the Old World

termites' hills. Possibly the birds derive some protection from interference by these curious associations. In New Zealand, some species of shearwaters share their burrows with a lizard, the tuatara. The shearwaters dig the burrows and allow the tuatara to use them. The lizard's contribution seems to be to keep the underground home free of insects. Abandoned woodpeckers' holes in huge saguaro cacti in the Arizona desert are a favourite nesting site of the tiny Elf Owl (*Micrathene whitneyi*). In Britain, Kestrels (*Falco tinnunculus*) will often occupy the deserted nests of crows and magpies.

Two strange species of birds known as bare-headed rockfowl live in the rain forests of West Africa; they are rarely seen by Europeans, and magical powers are attributed to them by Africans. For such large birds, they are remarkable in that they construct a nest of mud like that of a swallow, which they plaster to a rockface. The nest is not made exclusively of mud, but is interwoven with fibres and reinforced with small sticks around the rim. Several nests may be built close together on a rockface, usually seven feet or more from the ground. Owing to their large size, the nests collapse easily when wet, so have to be built below an overhanging rock to protect them from the rain.

The rarer of the two species, the Grey-necked Rockfowl (*Picathartes oreas*), is found only in Cameroon, while the more widely distributed White-necked Rockfowl (*Picathartes gymnocephalus*) inhabits Sierra Leone, Liberia, Ghana, and Togo. The White-necked species has the bare skin of its head coloured yellow, with a circular black patch behind each eye; the bare skin of the head of the Grey-necked Rockfowl is red, blue, and black. Both species are very similar in size, measuring about fourteen inches in length from bill to tail, have long legs, and look unlike any other birds. Seldom flying, they progress about the forest floor by a series of hops.

Crested tree swifts build a tiny shallow cup made from flakes of bark and lichen glued together with saliva, which is barely big enough to contain their single egg. The nest is built on the side of a slender branch, which is usually bare of leaves. When the egg is being incubated, the nest is almost completely hidden by the sitting bird. The fledgling Crested Tree Swift (*Hemiprocne longipennis*) has a mottled plumage, making it virtually indistinguishable from the knots and lichens of the branch its nest is situated on. The crested tree swifts are a small group found in South East Asia and the western Pacific, and are less specialized than the true swifts.

The nest of the widely distributed Palm Swift (*Cypsiurus parvus*), is a small pad of feathers just large enough to hold the two eggs and glued to the underside of a palm leaf with saliva. The eggs are incubated in a vertical position by the swift, which clings to the nest with its claws.

Bird's nest soup, sometimes called the 'caviar of the East' is made from the nests of certain swiftlets (*Collocalia* spp.) in the same group. Highest prized of all are the nests composed entirely of salivary secretion; others are mixed with feathers or vegetable matter and are not so highly esteemed. Regarded by the Chinese and other Asians as a delicacy, the nests are of negligible nutritional value and when eaten

Examining the mud nest of the White-necked Rockfowl; it builds below an overhanging rock-face to protect the nest from the rain which would otherwise wash it away

The nest of the Palm Swift is just a small pad of feathers glued to the underside of a palm leaf

Built from moss woven together with
hair, spiders' webs and lichens,
the nest of the Long-tailed Tit may be
lined with as many as 2,000 feathers

top
A hovering female hummingbird is about
to feed her youngster which has almost
outgrown the tiny nest made from
plant-down and bud-scales
held together with spiders' webs

above right
A Kingfisher leaving its nesting burrow
in the steep bank of a river

Of all birds nests, none compare with
that built by the aptly named
tailorbirds of South East Asia

Robins are well known for their habit
of nesting in curious places; this bird
has nested in an old metal jug
wedged in the fork of a branch

alone are almost tasteless. Collecting the edible nests
in the dark caves can be a hazardous occupation.
Usually this task is carried out by a man with a set of
connecting bamboo poles with a blade attached to the
end for scraping the nests from the cave walls. The
man with the cutting instrument climbs about the
walls and ledges detaching the nests and has an
assistant on the ground below who collects them.

The enclosed nest constructed by the Hammerhead
is so strong that it is able to support the weight of a
man standing on it. Placed in the fork of a tree fifteen
to sixty feet or more from the ground and usually
close to water, the nest is made from sticks and other
vegetation mixed with mud. There is a small entrance
hole at the side with a tunnel connected to the
nesting chamber, which may be four feet across and
lined with mud and dung. Hammerheads take about a
month to build their huge nest and there is a common
belief that other birds assist them by bringing nesting
materials while they are building. This, however, is
untrue, for the nest is the work of the two
Hammerheads only. The nesting chamber is well
insulated from the sun, and when the Hammerhead is
incubating its three to six white eggs, a constant
temperature is maintained within. The entrance
tunnel is usually impregnable to snakes and small
mammalian predators, but barn owls often get in and
eject the owners.

Hammerheads are confined to the Ethiopian
region, where they frequent marshes, mangrove
swamps, tidal creeks, and the banks of rivers and
streams. They are a small, dull-brown relation of the
storks. A similar structure to the Hammerheads' is
built by the Rufous Ovenbird (*Furnarius rufus*), a
small bird which inhabits parts of South America.

Instead of using their own body heat to incubate
their eggs, the megapodes or mound-builders lay their
eggs in holes in the ground or in mounds of rotting
vegetable matter, leaving the eggs to be incubated by
natural heat. One member of this small fowl-like
family, the Malee Fowl (*Leipoa ocellata*) of the
Australian bush, builds a mound of sand and
vegetable matter which may measure about fifteen
feet in diameter and be four feet high. The eggs which
may number as many as thirty-five are laid in a hole
dug in the centre of the mound, and the rotting
vegetation generates enough heat to incubate the
eggs. The mound is constantly attended by the male
who regulates the heat by either adding or scraping
away sand so that 92 degrees Fahrenheit is
maintained during incubation. He spends almost his
entire year either building or maintaining the mound.
When the young hatch they have to struggle to the
surface unassisted by their parents and are
immediately able to fend for themselves.

Most ingenious of all nests are those constructed by
a small group of warblers which live in South East
Asia. Aptly named tailorbirds, they have long straight
bills and long tails, which they hold erect like a wren.
They select two large leaves, and with their bills
puncture holes around the edges of them. They then
collect strands of cottony fluff, which they push
through the holes of the two leaves, so that they are
drawn together. In the little pocket which is formed,
the tailorbird constructs its nest proper, composed of
fine grasses and plant-down.

White Storks like to nest high whether in open country or in cities. In many places in Europe this species is thought to bring good luck and is encouraged and carefully protected.

left
A Great Reed Warbler on its nest in a reed bed. This species resembles the Reed Warbler but is much larger and the eye stripe more pronounced.

below left
Each unconcerned about the other— a Dabchick or Little Grebe sits on its floating nest, while not more than a yard away a warbler also incubates

Nocturnal Birds

The vast majority of birds are entirely diurnal, confining their activities to the hours of daylight and sleeping by night. A small minority, however, are nocturnal and live in the reverse order. Best known of these birds of the night are the owls, a family which occurs throughout the world except in Antarctica and a few isolated oceanic islands. Other examples are the Oilbird (*Steatornis caripensis*), a species peculiar to the Neotropical region, the kiwis and the nightjars. Other groups again, like many of the petrels, are nocturnal in their nesting activities but mainly search for food during the day. Most ducks and waders are chiefly birds of the daylight hours, but they will also show considerable activity during the hours of darkness. In what may be an adaptation to the need to leave the day free for feeding, many species which are otherwise diurnal migrate by night.

Most species that are nocturnal or crepuscular–that is, active in the dim light of dusk and dawn–exploit a source of food which is also active at this time. This is true of many owls which feed upon nocturnal rodents, and nightjars which feed on insects that fly in the twilight. For other species, like the flightless kiwis, the darkness probably constitutes a form of defence from diurnal predators. This is also the case with the petrels, which are ungainly on land but must visit it in order to breed. Diurnal species migrating by night are also less likely to fall prey to predators. The night-time activities of many of the ducks and waders are governed by the state of the tides. Why the fruit-eating Oilbird should be nocturnal is not so easy to answer!

Species which are active during the hours of darkness require some form of concealment to remain hidden from likely enemies while they are resting during the day. In many instances they may spend the day in holes or burrows used for nesting, and sometimes also for roosting outside the breeding season. Concealment may also be achieved by resting in dense foliage or ground cover, or, more commonly, by virtue of cryptic coloration which enables a bird to merge into its background. The colour of the plumage of owls, for example, is very varied, but tends towards patterns that make them less conspicuous by day. Cryptic coloration is also exhibited by nightjars, frogmouths and related species. In their usual prone resting position on the ground, many nightjars resemble fallen pieces of wood; the frogmouths and their allies more usually perch in trees and adopt a posture that simulates a broken branch. All these birds close their eyes when in the presence of an intruder and remain motionless.

Although, contrary to popular belief, owls cannot see in total darkness, they nevertheless have remarkably good eyesight at night. As a further aid to nocturnal hunting, their hearing is very acute. The characteristic facial discs are shaped to trap sounds like the parabolic reflectors which sound technicians use and each ear is differently shaped and located asymmetrically on either side of the head. Their acute hearing enables them to locate and capture prey by sound alone if necessary. Owls are also able to turn their heads right round in each direction, which helps them locate sounds without continually changing

Despite its barred appearance this owl, which is common in many parts of Africa, is called the Spotted Eagle Owl

An American Barn Owl alighting with its catch

position. In addition, owls have particularly soft feathers which enable them to fly silently, helping them to pounce unsuspected on their prey. Not all owls are completely noctural hunters, however, for many will also hunt by day.

There are about 130 species of owls, divided into two main groups: the barn owls (*Tytonidae*) and the so-called typical owls (*Strigidae*). They vary greatly in size, the tiny Elf Owl (*Micrathene whitneyi*) being about the size of a sparrow, while the Great Eagle Owl (*Bubo bubo*) is almost that of an eagle. The barn owl group comprises about ten species, and sometimes includes the Bay Owl (*Phodilus badius*) of Asia and a related African species, the Congo Bay Owl (*Phodilus progoginei*). Barn owls are easily recognizable, for they have a heart-shaped facial disc and long, slender legs. Their eyes are rather small for nocturnal birds, but their hearing is exceptionally good. The Barn Owl (*Tyto alba*), which occurs in the British Isles, is an almost world-wide ranging species, with over thirty recognizable geographical forms. In Australia as many as five different species occur, while in New Zealand and the oceanic islands barn owls are absent.

Just over a dozen different species of owl are known from Europe, including the huge Great Eagle Owl, but the commonest of the British owls is the Tawny Owl (*Strix aluco*), a species which even occurs in parts of central London. Owls feed almost exclusively on animal life, small ground-living rodents being the most widely eaten prey. In Africa and southern Asia there occur a number of owls that catch and eat fish. The Asian species also take small mammals, birds, reptiles, crabs and insects. Female owls are normally slightly larger and heavier than males, but both sexes usually have similar coloured plumage. A notable exception is the Snowy Owl (*Nyctea scandiaca*), for the plumage of the male is usually pure white, while that of the female has bold dark barring.

The Oilbird is unique both in its behaviour and in the fact that it is the only nocturnal fruit-eating bird. It is placed in a family of its own alongside the nightjars and their allies. Its plumage is a rich brown, with some black barring and a scattering of white spots which are particularly conspicuous on parts of the wings. Its appearance is halfway between that of a big nightjar and a hawk. It has a strongly hooked bill, long wings with a span of just over a yard, a medium-length tail and small, weak legs.

Oilbirds occur in northern South America and Trinidad. They are gregarious and spend all day crouching on ledges in the caves where they live. At night they fly out and feed on the fruit of various forest trees which they pluck by means of their hooked bill while on the wing. The Oilbird lacks a crop, and is said to bring the fruit back to the caves in its stomach whole, digesting it during the day. The seeds from the fruit are regurgitated and fall on to lower ledges or to the floor, forming a thick coating.

Most outstanding of the Oilbird's attributes is its ability to fly through the pitch-dark, narrow, twisting caves with unfailing accuracy; sometimes its roosting place can be as much as half a mile from the entrance. When flying through the caves, it emits a stream of evenly spaced clicks or snapping sounds with a

A Barn Owl with a rodent grasped in its bill. This species has an almost world-wide distribution.

left
A Great Eagle Owl with its two chicks. This eagle owl occurs in some of the more remote parts of Europe.

far left
Mammals, birds, reptiles and insects are all eaten by the Great Eagle Owl

A Little Owl about to enter its nesting
hole with an insect in its bill

below
A fine study of a female Snowy Owl;
the plumage of the smaller male
is usually pure white. This species
lives in the barren Arctic wastes,
where it feeds mainly on lemmings.

frequency of about 7,000 cycles per second. These enable it, presumably from the delay in the echo, to locate and thus avoid the walls. The system it uses resembles that employed by bats; similarly, if its ears are plugged, the Oilbird can no longer navigate in the dark. In addition to the clicking sounds, Oilbirds also utter very loud screaming and snarling calls. The local name Guacharo is Spanish for 'one who cries and laments'. A chorus of several hundred birds in a large cave can be almost deafening. When flying outside the caves at night, they utter occasional harsh cries, but not the echo-locating clicks. Their eyes are rather large and highly sensitive, with excellent night vision which is used when flying about outside the caves.

The Oilbird or Guacharo's nest is a mound with a shallow depression on top, placed on a ledge high on the cave wall. It is made from pulpy regurgitated fruit, disgorged seeds and the bird's own droppings. The two to four white eggs which are laid are incubated by both sexes. When they hatch after thirty-three days the young are covered with a little sparse down, which is later replaced by another coat of down. They become extremely fat, and just prior to their feathers starting to grow may weigh almost twice as much as an adult bird. It is at this stage that the local Indians harvest them for their fat, which when boiled down yields a good quality oil. This is the reason for the English name, Oilbird.

The ability to fly into dark caves and to nest in them successfully is also found in the Black-nest Swiftlet (*Collocalia maxima*) of South East Asia. This swiftlet nests in dark caves, often in vast numbers, and also utters a rapid succession of clicking notes whose rebounding echoes enable it to navigate in total darkness. A closely related species, the White-bellied Swiftlet (*Collocalia esculenta*), which inhabits only the mouths of caves has been found to have no echo technique.

Most nightjars are crepuscular or nocturnal in their habits. They feed chiefly on insects, and to enable them to catch their food on the wing they have an extremely wide gape. Many species also have long bristles at the base of their bills which enable them to trap their prey even more effectively. During the day they rest quietly and are difficult to detect owing to their cryptic coloration, which is usually brown or grey, mottled, streaked or barred with various other shades. Their plumage is soft, loose and fluffy like that of the owls. The nightjars and their allies are almost world-wide in distribution, but are notably absent from the most northern parts of America, Europe and Asia, as well as southern South America and New Zealand. North Americans call them goatsuckers and nighthawks. Nightjars are to be found in a variety of habitats, more usually in open stretches in wooded areas or forests, and sometimes in deserts. Normally they perch on the ground or lengthwise on a branch. In many parts of Africa they are frequently encountered sitting on roads at night. One theory for this behaviour is that the clear, flat roads are ideal places for hunting insects.

The family falls into two main groups, one of which is restricted to the New World. The nighthawks which form this latter group are distinguished by their lack of rictal bristles at the base of the bill.

More than half of all nightjar species belong to the same genus as the Nightjar (*Caprimulgus europaeus*) occurring in the British Isles, and many of them are like it in plumage. The 'churring' or 'jarring' call of this species is the origin of its English name, while 'goatsucker' is a translation of the Latin *Caprimulgus* which refers to the ancient superstition that these birds sucked the milk of goats and sheep during the night. North American representatives include the Whip-poor-will (*Caprimulgus vociferus*) and Chuck-will's Widow (*Caprimulgus carolinensis*). One American species, the Poor-will (*Phalaenoptilus nuttallii*) has been recorded hibernating among crevices in rocky cliffs during the cold insect-free winter, instead of migrating to warmer parts as most species do. During hibernation their body temperature drops from a normal 102 degrees Fahrenheit to about 65 degrees Fahrenheit, while their breathing slows to almost nothing, and the digestive processes cease. The fact that these birds hibernate was not believed by ornithologists until the early 1940s, although the Indians of Arizona had known of it for centuries.

In a few species, particularly in Africa, the male exhibits remarkable elongated feathers in the wings or tail during the breeding season. For example, the male Standard-winged Nightjar (*Macrodipteryx longipennis*) has the shaft of one feather of each wing greatly elongated and unfeathered for part of its length, only to be feathered again at the terminal portion. In flight it is most conspicuous and has the appearance of being pursued by two moths which follow its every twist and turn. This species is an intertropical migrant, for it breeds in the southern part of its range across the middle of Africa, moving north and east outside the breeding season.

When in breeding dress, the inner primaries of the male Pennant-winged Nightjar (*Semeiophorus vexillarius*) grow into fluttering pennants of two feet or more in length. Displayed during the courtship flight, the pennants may take the place of the calls which other nightjars use when courting, for it appears to be voiceless. It is another intertropical migrant which, unlike many of its relatives, hunts and flies freely by day. The male Long-tailed Nightjar (*Scotornis climacurus*) has its central pair of tail feathers greatly elongated during the breeding season.

Allied to the nightjars are the frogmouths, owlet frogmouths and potoos. The frogmouths are a group of a dozen species, confined to the Oriental and Australasian regions. Frogmouths have protective colouring and soft plumage like nightjars, but differ in their habits and structural characteristics. Their bills are large, flattened, triangular and sharply hooked. To a large extent they have forsaken the aerial feeding habit; instead, they capture most of their prey on the ground or from branches. In Australia the big Tawny Frogmouth (*Podargus strigoides*) will sometimes even catch mice. The dumpy little owlet frogmouths of Australia and New Guinea, the Moluccas and New Caledonia are closely related to the frogmouths, but the largest is no more than twelve inches long. Their feeding habits seem to be intermediate between those of the frogmouths and nightjars, for they both capture prey on the ground and hunt for night-flying insects on the

A Nightjar hovering. They have
an especially wide gape
and catch insects in flight.

wing. For this reason they are sometimes called
'moth owls' in Australia.

The strangely named potoos are a small group of
five species confined to the Neotropical region which
in general appearance and coloration resemble the
frogmouths. 'Potoo' is the creole name given to one of
the species from its distinctive call. They become
active at night, feeding on flying insects which they
capture after the fashion of flycatchers. They sit
quietly on a favourite perch and fly out to grab the
insects as they flit by, returning to eat them at their
observation point.

In Africa and parts of the Far East lives the Bat
Hawk (*Machaerhamphus alcinus*), a bird of prey that
feeds chiefly on bats which it hunts at dusk as they
emerge from caves or buildings. Apart from bats it
also eats swallows, martins and large insects and in
the Far East it frequently haunts the mouths of caves
inhabited by swiftlets. In order to hunt its aerial prey
successfully, it requires wide open spaces such as
those found over forest pools and broad rivers, and it
is not averse to visiting human habitations, to
hunting over railway stations, or even large open
gardens around buildings. In its general appearance
the Bat Hawk is like a large falcon, with a wide gape
and very large eyes adapted to its nocturnal habits.

Very swift on the wing, the Bat Hawk catches its

prey in full flight with its feet. It commonly swallows
its prey while in the air and, in the case of bats, whole
including the wings. In Africa, because of the
nocturnal habits of bats, it probably hunts for only
about half an hour each day. In the Far East,
however, where a large proportion of swiftlets are
included in its diet, it is probably able to hunt for
longer. To enable it to catch sufficient food to subsist
in the short hunting time available, prey must be very
numerous. As a result of its highly specialized feeding
habits it is a rare bird throughout most of its range,
but is locally quite common.

During the day the Bat Hawk sits quietly in a large
tree, seldom flying about in daylight. It leaves its
resting place just before dusk, and hunts until the
light has almost gone; it will also hunt in the early
morning. The Bat Hawk nests in trees, and one or
sometimes two eggs are laid; these are white with a
few grey markings. Both parents feed the nestlings,
apparently only bringing food to the nest for a short
time before dark. During this time the food is brought
at very rapid intervals.

Another bird of prey that hunts bats is the Bat
Falcon (*Falco rufigularis*) which is often active at
twilight as bats are entering and leaving caves; it also
hunts moths at dusk. It is a New World species and
varies its diet with hummingbirds, swallows and
swifts. Extremely agile in flight, it will hunt either
from a perch or on the wing.

On the whole, birds of prey hunt by day, and
although a few species like the Bat Hawk and Bat
Falcon are crepuscular, none is truly nocturnal. The
Bat Falcon and, most nocturnal of all, the Bat Hawk
are dependent upon vision when hunting. Vultures
have been recorded feeding on carcasses on moonlit
nights, having first descended to the ground by
daylight, while in Australia a species of kite is known
to catch mice by moonlight.

For many years after the arrival of the first
European traders and settlers in New Zealand, the
unobtrusive kiwis remained unnoticed. During the
day these flightless birds remain hidden in burrows or
other hiding places in the thick swampy forest,
emerging at night to forage. Today, the kiwis' forest
habitat has been much reduced, but they are still
plentiful in suitable localities. Being extremely shy
and retiring, as well as nocturnal, they are seldom
seen by human beings. The three species are all
dull-coloured birds, about the size of a large chicken,
with short powerful legs and long thin slightly
down-curved bills. The females of all three species
are larger than the males. Kiwis nest in underground burrows, and the one or two large white eggs
which may take as long as seventy-seven days to
hatch are incubated by the male alone. It has been
observed that the young of the North Island Kiwi
(*Apteryx australis mantelli*) are not fed during the
first six days in the nest, and when they do leave they
pick up their own food, helped by the male who clears
patches of ground for them.

Kiwis are the only birds to have the nostril
apertures at the tip of the bill. Because of this they
probably have a keen sense of smell, lacking in most
other birds, which they use to find earthworms,
insects, and fallen berries. Their eyes are small
suggesting poorly developed sight.

The nocturnal flightless Kiwi, a native
of New Zealand. Note the long bill with
the nostrils near the tip which
is used to probe for insects.

The Night Heron, seen here at its nest,
roosts silently during the day among
the branches of a tree or other dense
cover and emerges at dusk to feed

A Bat Falcon resting during the day-time;
it hunts at twilight, often varying
its diet of bats with hummingbirds,
swifts and swallows

During the day the Tawny Frogmouth
avoids detection by simulating a dead
branch

right
The wide gape and the large, flattened,
triangular and sharply hooked bill
of the Australian Tawny Frogmouth
are particularly well illustrated
by this photograph

above
A tiny Elf Owl only 5½ ins in length
peers from its nesting hole
in a giant saguaro cactus

right
Using its cryptic coloration
to full advantage, a Nightjar nests among
some woodland undergrowth

below
A Tawny Owl with a rodent grasped in its
foot perches on the edge of its nest;
two white eggs are clearly visible

Birds
of the
Oceans

Some birds spend almost their entire lives at sea. The only time many of them come to land is to nest. At sea most of them have few natural enemies and, contrary to what might be expected, life is comparatively safe. Nearly all of them are long-lived and have a low reproductive rate. It is common for the females of several oceanic families to lay only one egg each. Sea birds on the whole tend to have long periods of adolescence before they can breed. With the King Penguin (*Aptenodytes patagonica*) this period may be as long as seven years, while for one species of albatross it can be as long as nine years, during which time it has been suggested that the young bird may never visit land. Without exception, all oceanic birds are colonial nesters.

Almost a hundred species go to make up the order Procellariiformes, which embraces the albatrosses, typical petrels, shearwaters, storm petrels, and diving petrels. Together with the penguins they show the greatest adaptation among birds to life at sea. The species of the order Procellariiformes are characterized by the tubular structure of their nostrils and are commonly called 'tubenoses'. The purpose of their distinctive nostrils is not fully understood, but they probably use them to get rid of excess salt, or, perhaps to help them locate by smell either their food, each other or their breeding places.

The albatrosses are the largest of the tubenoses; all of the thirteen or fourteen species are goose-sized with long narrow wings. Their plumage is mainly white or brown, usually with some dark brown or black on the wings and often on the back and tail. They are notable for their spectacular powers of flight, for they are able to glide for long distances on motionless wings. Albatrosses are principally birds of the southern seas, from the tropics south to the Antarctic, but a few occur in the North Pacific and occasionally southern species wander into northern waters. Often they will travel great distances; one ringed bird has been recorded some 6,000 miles from where it was first found. They frequently follow ships, and superstitious mariners have long thought them to be the spirits of sailors swept overboard in gales.

With a wing-spread of perhaps eleven feet or more, the Wandering Albatross (*Diomedea exulans*), if not quite the largest flying bird, certainly has the biggest wing-span. A bird of the southern seas, it breeds on such islands as Tristan da Cunha and South Georgia, and the Kerguelen and Auckland Islands. The Laysan Albatross (*Diomedea immutabilis*) is a North Pacific species, while the Royal Albatross (*Diomedea epomophora*) is familiar in New Zealand waters.

Albatrosses usually nest in large colonies on remote islands. Both sexes share the duties of incubating the single whitish egg, which may take from two to three months to hatch. Unlike most of their close relatives which breed in underground burrows, albatrosses nest in the open, the nest usually being a mere scrape in the ground, or a mound of earth or plant material. All albatrosses have quite a spectacular courtship display which may involve dancing, accompanied by wing spreading, bowing and bill snapping. With some species, such as the Wandering and Royal Albatrosses, the youngster takes so long to raise that these albatrosses are able to nest only every other year. The downy young, of

A Buller's Albatross glides over the sea on its long, thin, motionless wings

With wings outstretched, a male Wandering Albatross arrives back at the nest. This species has a wing-spread of perhaps 11 ft.

A Rockhopper Penguin settles down
to brood its egg. This species is
so named because it hops along with
its two feet held together.

An Emperor Penguin with its
two-month-old chick. The male Emperor
incubates its single egg
for about 64 days.

This fine study of a Giant Petrel on its nest illustrates particularly well the tubular structure of the nostrils which gives the 'tubenoses' their name

A Black-browed Albatross feeding its chick on regurgitated food

some albatrosses at least, are able to eject oil from their stomachs as a means of defence. Many other tubenoses are also capable of doing this.

By far the largest group of tubenoses are the fifty or more species of typical petrels and shearwaters. Included in this group is the Fulmar (*Fulmarus glacialis*) which breeds around the coasts of the British Isles. The Fulmar, which has more than one colour phase, is a species which has markedly increased in numbers over the years. Its increase can doubtless be attributed to the way it has readily taken to scavenging.

The Cape Pigeon (*Daption capensis*), or more correctly the Cape or Pintado Petrel, is a bird which is common in the southern seas. It has a most distinctive chequered black and white plumage. Little is known of the feeding habits of this species, but it seems likely that it eats mainly plankton. Like other petrels it often follows ships, perhaps to feed on the plankton the ships disturb, but more probably to collect scraps thrown overboard. It also follows fishing and whaling vessels and feeds on their refuse.

Both the previous species normally nest on cliffs. The Manx Shearwater (*Puffinus puffinus*), which breeds on many islands off the Atlantic coasts of the British Isles, nests in burrows. Like many of its relatives its plumage is basically black above and white below. Sweeping low over the water, the Manx Shearwater glides with its long graceful outspread wings curving first one side, then the other.

Most famous of this Shearwater's nesting colonies around the British coast are those on Skokholm and Skomer off Pembrokeshire in South Wales. Usually the nesting burrows are excavated in soft soil. Sometimes the nests join up to form a maze of tunnels that may be inhabited by Storm Petrels (*Hydrobates pelagicus*), Puffins (*Fratercula arctica*) or even rabbits. At their nesting colonies the shearwaters are strictly nocturnal and all comings and goings take place during darkness. A single egg is laid which hatches some seven to eight weeks later. For a few days after it has hatched the chick is brooded by its parents, then it is left alone during the day and fed by night for a further two months. By this time it is usually very fat, and its thick grey down is being replaced by its first feathers. It is now abandoned by its parents and may remain in the burrow for a further two weeks. During the last few days the young Manx Shearwater leaves the nest at night to exercise its wings before finally going to sea.

When they are nesting, adult shearwaters may travel hundreds of miles away from their breeding places in search of food. They feed largely on fish such as sardines and possibly young herrings. Ringing recoveries have shown that birds which breed in British waters not only disperse for hundreds of miles along the coasts of Europe to seek food in the breeding season, but also spend the winter off the east coast of South America. In addition to the main race breeding in the North Atlantic there are a number of races of this shearwater breeding elsewhere.

The tiny storm petrels are the smallest of the sea birds. They frequently follow ships, and sailors call them 'Mother Carey's chickens' which is probably a corruption of 'Mater Cara', the Divine Virgin, who is

An Antarctic Petrel wings its way
across the southern seas

A Manx Shearwater photographed at night
by flashlight. At their nesting colonies
the shearwaters are strictly nocturnal,
and all comings and goings take
place during darkness.

the guardian of all seamen. Most of them are chiefly
black or dark brown, usually with a conspicuous
white patch on the rump which, together with their
small size, makes them readily recognizable. They are
sometimes encountered singly, but more often in
small scattered flocks, usually flying just above the
water, with a fluttering and erratic flight, feeding on
small organisms which they snatch from the water's
surface.

Wilson's Petrel (*Oceanites oceanicus*) breeds all
round Antarctica and winters throughout the tropics,
sometimes wandering into northern waters. It it one
of the most abundant birds in the world, possibly even
the most abundant. At close quarters, it can be
distinguished from all similar species by the yellow
webs between its black toes, and from most others by
the possession of a square rather than forked tail.
Another of the twenty to twenty-two species of storm
petrels, known simply as the Storm Petrel
(*Hydrobates pelagicus*), breeds on the coasts of the
eastern North Atlantic, including parts of the
British Isles and the Mediterranean.

The diving petrels of the Southern Hemisphere
more closely resemble certain of the northern auks,
particularly the Little Auk (*Plautus alle*), than their
true relatives. The resemblance, however, is only
superficial, for the two groups are unrelated. It is an
excellent example of parallel evolution, for the diving
petrels also behave in many ways like the auks. The
four or five species are very alike in appearance,
differing mainly in the structure of their bills.

Diving petrels feed principally on crustaceans, as
well as small fish that they catch underwater. They
tend to be more plentiful in the waters near their
breeding places, and are not encountered far out at
sea as often as other petrels. Most widely distributed
of the group is the Common Diving Petrel
(*Pelecanoides urinatrix*) which occurs from the
Atlantic coast of southern South America, eastwards
across the South Atlantic and Indian Ocean to
Australia and New Zealand.

Best known of all oceanic birds are the penguins,
for they are seen by the millions of people who each
year visit zoos and bird gardens around the world.
These rather comic-looking flightless creatures make
wonderful exhibits and few zoos are without them. In
captivity they are exceedingly entertaining and
appear quite at home, but really they are being seen
at a disadvantage. They are supremely suited to life
in the water and it is here that they are seen at their
best. In the water they move with power and agility
propelled by their flippers and using their feet and
tail to steer. It has been estimated that some species
are able to travel in excess of twenty-five miles per
hour underwater. They are capable of propelling
themselves fast enough to leap several feet clear of
the water, to land on shelves of ice or rocks which
would otherwise be inaccessible. On land, some
species are able to run, but others can only hop or
waddle. Adelie Penguins (*Pygoscelis adeliae*) can
sometimes outrun a man in soft, loose snow. Some
penguins will often travel across snow by flopping
down on their bellies and 'tobogganing' along, using
their feet and flippers to gather speed.

Penguins inhabit the seas and coasts of the Southern
Hemisphere. All are highly gregarious and feed on

fish, cuttlefish, and crustaceans. In the sea their main enemies are the Leopard Seal and the Killer Whale; there is a record of eighteen Adelie Penguins being found in the stomach of a single seal. Their eggs and young are taken by such birds as sheathbills and skuas. Penguins are monogamous and long-lived, often pairing for life.

Of the seventeen to eighteen species the largest is the Emperor Penguin (*Aptenodytes forsteri*); four feet in length and weighing between fifty and a hundred pounds, it is the largest and heaviest sea bird. Next in size is the King Penguin (*Aptenodytes patagonicus*), about ten inches shorter and more slightly built, weighing between thirty and forty pounds. The former breeds only on the Antarctic continent while the King breeds on South Georgia, Kerguelen, Macquarie, and other islands in the Antarctic seas. These two species of penguin make no nest but instead incubate in a standing position with the single egg held on top of their feet and covered by a pouch-like fold of abdominal skin. They are able to shuffle about for short distances with the egg, and later with the chick while it is small enough.

Emperor Penguins are one of the few birds which begin their breeding season in the autumn rather than spring. They rear their chicks during the long Antarctic winter to ensure that they reach independence during the summer and have a better chance of survival. Only the males incubate. The egg takes approximately sixty-four days to hatch and during this time they sometimes huddle together in huge packs to conserve heat. Meanwhile, the females are in the open sea which may be fifty or even a

A Southern Skua
fearlessly attacking an enemy

Penguins are supremely suited to life
in the water, where they move with power
and agility propelled by their flippers
and using their feet and tail to steer

A Common Tern returning to its eggs.
Outside the breeding season the bill
of this species becomes darker
and its forehead white.

top
Covered with brown down, a King Penguin
chick stands beside one of its parents.
It will be some time before it loses
its down and is as tall as the adult.

above left
Adelie Penguins normally lay two eggs
which hatch after about 35 days.
Both sexes help gather the pile of stones
which form the nest, and there is much
stealing of stones from other nests.

above right
Four Guillemots perched on a rocky ledge
overlooking the sea; the two birds
with a narrow white line extending
back from around the eye
belong to the 'Bridled' form

hundred miles from the nesting colony. When the chick first emerges from the egg it is fed by the male with a secretion from the crop, but later the female returns from the sea and cares for it. With the arrival of his mate the male goes off to sea and feeds for the first time for perhaps three months. The egg of the King Penguin, which takes about ten days less to hatch, is incubated by both male and female.

The Adelie Penguin (*Pygoscelis adeliae*), which is widely distributed around the coasts of Antarctica and also breeds on the South Orkneys and South Shetlands, builds a nest of stones and lays two eggs. Males and females usually pair for many years and are faithful to their old nesting sites, seeming able to find their old site each year even if it is covered by snow. Both sexes help gather the pile of stones which form the nest, and there is much stealing of stones from other nests. The two eggs hatch out after an average of thirty-five days. During incubation both sexes go for long periods without food while their mate goes off to feed at sea. The male Adelie Penguin does the first spell of incubation and may fast for as long as six weeks, losing forty per cent of its body weight. For the first month one parent always remains at the nest with the young, but later the chicks are left by themselves and gather into groups or crèches of 100 or more birds.

Smallest of the penguins is the Little Blue or Fairy Penguin (*Eudyptula minor*), which measures sixteen inches in length from bill to tail so that it stands only about a foot high. It is found on the coasts and islands of southern Australia from Perth to Brisbane, around Tasmania, New Zealand, and the Chatham Islands. Some species like the Rockhopper (*Eudyptes crestatus*) and Macaroni Penguins (*Eudyptes chrysolophus*) have ornamental yellow plumes beginning over the eye and falling down the back of the head. The Rockhopper Penguin breeds in New Zealand, as well as on Tristan da Cunha, Gough Island, the Falkland Islands, and various islands of the Antarctic. Its name is taken from its habit of progressing along by a series of hops with its feet held together.

The Jackass or Black-footed Penguin (*Spheniscus demersus*) breeds in burrows and hollows on small islands off the west coast of South Africa. It is very plentiful on and around these islands, where it breeds mainly in the late summer and early winter, but quite a number of birds can be found nesting at almost any time of the year. The Jackass and the very similar Humboldt Penguin (*Spheniscus humboldti*) are the two species of penguins most commonly kept in zoos. The latter species breeds on the coasts of Chile northwards to Peru.

Related to the Jackass and Humboldt Penguins is the small Galapagos Penguin (*Spheniscus mendiculus*). It is restricted to the archipelago of the same name and is the only penguin to reach as far north as the Equator. It appears to breed only on the islands of Albermarle and Narborough, although Charles Island is occasionally visited; it was probably formerly more widely distributed in the archipelago. It usually chooses a nesting site in a hole in the lava rock and lays two eggs.

The Auk family of the northern seas embraces some twenty-two species. They are known by an almost

Smallest of the penguins is the Little Blue or Fairy Penguin which is seen here emerging from its nesting burrow

Two Humboldt Penguins looking as though they are holding hands

The diving petrels of the Southern Hemisphere more closely resemble certain of the northern auks, particularly the Little Auk shown here, than their true relatives

bewildering variety of names, the same species often being called by a different name on either side of the Atlantic. In North America the Razorbill (*Alca torda*) is known as the Razor-billed Auk, the Guillemot (*Uria aalge*) as the Common Murre, Brünnich's Guillemot (*Uria lomvia*) as the Thick-billed Murre and the Little Auk (*Plautus alle*) as the Dovekie.

Fish and marine invertebrates, especially crustaceans, are the main food of the group. Underwater, they use their wings for propulsion and the feet for steering, obtaining their food by pursuit. In flight, they fly rapidly and directly with fast wing beats. Most of them nest colonially.

Both the Guillemot and the Razorbill, which breed around the coasts of the British Isles, make no nest but usually lay their single egg on a bare rocky ledge. The Puffin (*Fratercula arctica*) nests in underground burrows. This species occurs in the North Atlantic, but is replaced in the North Pacific by the Horned Puffin (*Fratercula corniculata*) and the Tufted Puffin (*Lunda cirrhata*), while the Little Auk is replaced by the small auklets.

Apart from the more oceanic birds, there are many others which spend much of their lives at sea without ever being too far from land. Some search for food at sea during the day but roost on land at night, while many only come to land to nest, or perhaps during bad weather. Species such as the divers or loons live on lakes, ponds and rivers in the summer, but in the winter are essentially marine, frequenting sea coasts. They are a small group confined to the Northern Hemisphere. Skilled at swimming and diving, they feed chiefly on fish.

Gannets and boobies are exclusively marine, but are offshore rather than oceanic birds. They are represented on the coasts of all the continents except Antarctica. There are nine species, of which the gannets live in temperate waters and the boobies in tropical waters. They feed mainly on fish but also eat squid. To capture their food, gannets and boobies plunge into the sea, with partly closed wings, sometimes from as high as 100 feet up. They strike the water with considerable force, and do not spear the fish as might be expected but grasp it in the bill.

Boobies are often robbed of their fish by frigate- or man-of-war-birds. The latter usually nest close to colonies of breeding boobies and other sea birds, in tropical waters, and as they return from the sea, force them to disgorge and then catch the food in mid-air. Frigatebirds are, however, capable of fishing for themselves. Flying fish are a favourite food; as the fish leap out of the water, the birds swoop down and catch them.

Tropicbirds are aptly named, for they seldom occur beyond the tropical seas. Except for the two long central tail feathers, which may exceed the length of the body, they resemble gulls in appearance. They nest mainly on oceanic and offshore islands and outside the breeding season wander the seas, where they tend to live solitarily or in pairs, feeding on small fish and squid. The only species with barred adult plumage, the Red-billed Tropicbird (*Phaethon aethereus*), extends from the Galapagos Islands through the Caribbean and Atlantic Ocean into the Red Sea and northern Indian Ocean.

A Razorbill flying in to join its three companions. This species which occurs on the coasts of the northern North Atlantic, is known as the Razor-billed Auk in North America.

A female Magnificent Frigatebird in flight; the male of this species lacks any white in its plumage

A Gannet stretches out its feet and fans its wings and tail as it prepares to land on a rocky ledge after a fishing trip at sea

Tropicbirds are aptly named, for they
seldom occur beyond the tropical seas.
Illustrated here is the largest species,
the Red-tailed Tropicbird, with
a juvenile in the foreground.

right
It is the exceptionally high quality down
with which the female Eider Duck lines
her nest that is used in
the manufacture of eiderdowns

One or other of the thirty or so species of cormorants occurs on coasts around most of the world and on many inland waters as well. The Cormorant (*Phalacrocorax carbo*), which is familiar around the coast of Britain, is the largest and most widely distributed species, with many races. Its range extends from eastern Canada and Greenland, through Europe, Africa, and much of Asia to Australia and New Zealand. In Australasia it is called the Black Cormorant, in North America the Great Cormorant, and elsewhere sometimes the Common Cormorant.

Cormorants feed largely on fish, and in the East have long been tamed and used for fishing. In Japan each fisherman works from a boat with a team of about a dozen birds, each on a leather tether. The birds are put over the side of the boat into the water and when they have a throat full of fish they are pulled back aboard. To prevent the cormorants from swallowing their catch a thong is tied around the base of the neck. The custom of using these birds for fishing dates back to the Sung dynasty (A.D. 960-1279) in China, and to the sixth century A.D. in Japan.

On the west coast of South America the guano or droppings of the Peruvian or Guanay Cormorant (*Phalacrocorax bougainvillii*) have been collected since the early nineteenth century. This nitrogenous substance is in demand as an organic fertilizer, and often brings high prices. In South Africa the guano of the Cape Cormorant (*Phalacrocorax capensis*) is collected.

Although popularly known as 'seagulls' most gulls are in fact coastal, or frequent inland waters and marshes. An exception is the almost circumpolar Kittiwake (*Larus tridactylus*) for, unlike most gulls, it regularly wanders the northern seas outside the breeding season. There are numerous records of ringed Kittiwakes crossing the Atlantic. Arctic Terns (*Sterna paradisaea*) which breed in the far north may migrate as far south as the coasts of Antarctica.

Among the marine ducks which inhabit the northern seas are the eiders and scoters. The males of the four species of eiders are very handsome birds, especially the male King Eider (*Somateria spectabilis*), while the females are all dull-coloured. It is the exceptionally high quality down of the female Eider (*Somateria mollissima*) that is used in the manufacture of eiderdowns. As in most other species of duck, the female plucks down from her breast to line the nest. Particularly in Iceland, the down is collected from the Eider's nest, apparently without harmful effect. The finest down is that taken a few days before the eggs hatch. Because of their economic value to farmers in Iceland, the Eiders are intensively encouraged and carefully protected.

The scoters are all very dull in colour; the males are predominantly black and the females brown. Like the eiders they tend to frequent offshore waters, coming on to land chiefly to breed, or during bad weather. Among the marine ducks of the southern seas are the steamer ducks. Two species of these heavily built diving ducks, which inhabit the coasts of southern South America and the Falkland Islands, are unable to fly.

An Arctic Tern returning to its nest and eggs. This species which breeds in the far north may migrate as far south as the coasts of Antarctica.

A Cormorant standing guard over its
two downy chicks; the sun is too hot
for the youngsters and they have
their bills held open

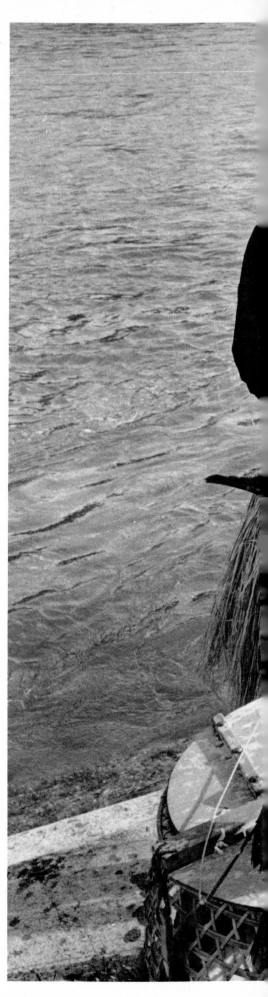

In the East cormorants have for thousands of years been tamed and used for fishing. Each fisherman works from a boat with a team of about a dozen birds, each on a tether. The birds are put over the side of the boat into the water and when they have a throat full of fish they are pulled back aboard. To prevent the cormorants from swallowing their catch a thong is tied around the base of the neck.

The Danger of Extinction

At some time or another, most of us have heard the expression 'as dead as the Dodo' used lightheartedly to describe something that has disappeared forever. The last unfortunate Dodo (*Raphus cucullatus*) probably disappeared in 1681. A huge, aberrant, flightless pigeon, it lived on the island of Mauritius in the Indian Ocean. Today our only reminders of the Dodo are a few bones, eggshells and drawings made at the time.

Including subspecies, over 120 other birds have vanished from the face of the earth since the last Dodo. The flightless Great Auk (*Pinguinus impennis*) of the North Atlantic disappeared around 1844. It was to this bird that the vernacular name 'penguin' was first applied, later to be transferred to the Southern Hemisphere group of birds known as penguins today. Another well-known example – perhaps the most spectacular of all – is the Passenger Pigeon (*Ectopistes migratorius*) of North America, for it existed in millions well into the nineteenth century and yet became extinct in the twentieth. At about the same time in North America the Carolina parrakeet (*Conuropsis carolinensis*) ceased to exist. More recent losses include the Pink-headed Duck (*Rhodonessa caryophyllacea*) of India, the Laysan Rail (*Porzanula palmeri*) which disappeared in 1944 and the Wake Island Rail (*Rallus wakensis*) a year later.

The extermination of the Dodo, like a number of other now extinct species, was brought about by man hunting it for food. Many Dodos were slaughtered by sailors from ships visiting Mauritius and a similar fate overtook the Great Auk. As well as being flightless, both had little fear of man and were, therefore, easily clubbed to death. The Wake Island Rail, which was confined to the island of the same name in the North Pacific, was common before the Second World War, but was very heavily preyed upon during the Japanese occupation of the island and did not recover. Other birds, like the small flightless Laysan Rail, have vanished or been greatly reduced because of predation or competition from cats, rats and other animals introduced into their habitat. Many have been driven to rarity or extinction by the disturbance or destruction of their natural habitat. Some other species have probably died out naturally.

Some birds previously thought to be extinct have been 'rediscovered', most famous of all perhaps being the Flightless Rail or Takahe (*Notornis mantelli*) of New Zealand. After an absence of half a century, the Takahe was rediscovered on the South Island of New Zealand in 1948. Trained ornithologists have since made an intensive study of this rail and have recorded much of its behaviour. Now carefully protected, there are probably in the order of 200 to 300 birds scattered in small groups over about 200 square miles of the island. A petrel called a Cahow (*Pterodroma cahow*) from Bermuda has also been rediscovered after being thought extinct, while in Puerto Rico, a Puerto Rico Whip-poor-will (*Caprimulgus noctitherus*) was found again in 1961, which happened to be the same year that the Noisy Scrub Bird (*Atrichornis clamosus*) was rediscovered in Australia. The latter had been thought extinct since 1920, while the Whip-poor-will was only known from

The Dodo, a wingless relative of the pigeon, stood about 2 ft high

Whooping Crane. These birds nest in Canada and winter in the Aransas National Wildlife Refuge in Texas.

bones and a skin. Recent reports suggest that the Crested Shelduck (*Tadorna cristata*) of Korea may also still be alive.

The rarest bird in the world today may well be the Ivory-billed Woodpecker (*Campephilus principalis*). Of the race found in the south-eastern U.S.A. it is unlikely that more than ten pairs remain, while the Cuban race may be down to as few as twelve or thirteen birds. A major factor in the decline of this woodpecker has been the relentless felling of trees in its favourite habitat. One of the largest and grandest of the world's woodpeckers, its plumage is a striking combination of black and white, with the male only having a red crest. Other endangered species in North America include the Whooping Crane (*Grus americanus*) and the California Condor (*Gymnogyps californianus*).

Whooping Cranes nest in Canada and winter in the Aransas National Wildlife Refuge in Texas. Because of the long migratory journey, this species has been particularly vulnerable to uncontrolled and ignorant shooting. However, much of its range is now controlled and losses during migration have dropped considerably. At the end of 1968 fifty birds wintered in the United States, to which number can be added the eighteen specimens in captivity. Twelve of the latter are at the Patuxent Wildlife Research Center in Maryland, and of these ten have been bred from eggs taken from the nests of the wild flock. The cranes lay two eggs but usually rear just a single chick; so one egg is taken from each nest and hatched artificially. It is hoped that a captive breeding stock will be built up so that eventually some can be released to augment the wild flock.

As a result of slaughter for feathers and meat, the population of the Trumpeter Swan (*Cygnus cygnus buccinator*) in the United States was down to sixty-nine in 1931, with an unknown number in Alaska. A few years later the United States Government acquired the Red Rock Lakes National Wildlife Refuge in south-west Montana, a traditional breeding ground which then contained over half of the Trumpeter Swans in the United States. With careful protection the swans increased until the early 1950s when their population began to level off. By then the refuge was supporting the maximum number of swans for which it could provide food and nesting territories, and surplus birds were transferred to other suitable areas. Today the population of the Trumpeter Swan is in excess of 5,000, which is a good example of what determined conservation can achieve.

Perilously few California Condors survive and for this species conservation may have come too late. A count in 1966 recorded only fifty-one individuals. The greatest losses among these fine birds in recent years have been from illegal shooting. Also its habitat is gradually diminishing as the human population continues to expand. California Condors do not mature until they are six years old and lay only a single egg every other year.

Another bird of prey in grave danger is the Monkey-eating Eagle (*Pithecophaga jefferyi*), a magnificent eagle from the Philippines. It is confined mainly to Mindanao Island, with a smaller population recently recorded from Luzon Island. At one time in the not too distant past it also lived on Leyte and Samar. It was from the latter island that the original specimen was described in 1897. The total population at present is estimated to be fewer than 100 birds. The huge Monkey-eating Eagle with its fierce appearance has always been much in

The Passenger Pigeon. The last of
its species, 'Martha', died in
the Cincinnati Zoo on 1st September, 1914

left
A pair of Great Auks from
Audubon's *Birds of America*.
This North Atlantic species
was last recorded in Iceland in 1844.

A Trumpeter Swan standing guard
alongside its sitting mate;
it is the largest of the world's swans

demand as a zoo exhibit. Recently, however, zoos
have become more conservation-minded and the
better ones have decided not to import any more of
these rare birds. Unfortunately, as this particular
threat to the species has dwindled, another more
curious threat has arisen: among the inhabitants of
the Philippines it has now become a status symbol to
own a mounted specimen of this eagle. As though
these threats to its existence were not enough, its
forest habitat is rapidly being destroyed both for
timber and cultivation. The future for the Monkey-
eating Eagle certainly looks very bleak.

The future of the Rothschild's Starling
(*Leucospar rothschildi*) has also been placed in
jeopardy by the demand for captive specimens. A
handsome bird, it is confined to the Indonesian
island of Bali, about 2,000 square miles in extent.
Its plumage is almost entirely pure white, except for
a black tip to the tail and wings and bare blue skin
around the eye. During the last decade particularly,
large numbers have found their way to zoos, private
aviculturists, and animal dealers–mainly in Europe
and the U.S.A.–and aviculturists have now
realized that the demands they have made have
greatly depleted the wild population. A census of
captive Rothschild's Starlings has been undertaken
and steps are now being taken to make this stock
self-sufficient by breeding. Fortunately, it is a species
that will breed readily in confinement.

Unlike the Monkey-eating Eagle and Rothschild's
Starling whose futures have been placed in
jeopardy by the demands of zoos, private
aviculturists and animal dealers, captivity may very
well prove to be the salvation of many of the
endangered pheasants. Most do well in confinement
and, of the world's forty-eight species, all but five
have at some time bred in captivity. Included among
those which have never reproduced in confinement
are the Chinese Monal (*Lophophorus Ihuysi*) and
Sclater's Monal (*Lophophorus sclateri*), both of
which are now almost extinct; many other rare
species, however, regularly hatch and rear young.
From these captive birds it is hoped that enough will
be bred to return some to the wild.

This process has already begun with Swinhoe's
Pheasant (*Lophura swinhoei*) of Taiwan, which was
first described by John Gould in 1862. Over a century
later, very little more is known about the range of
Swinhoe's Pheasant in the hill forests of Taiwan.
Though it may have been rare for a considerable
time, it is now likely that the wild stock is at a
dangerous level. There is, however, an estimated
captive population of about 600 birds. Many have
been bred at the Pheasant Trust in Norfolk. In 1967
Philip Wayre, Honorary Director of the Trust,
liberated half a dozen Norfolk-bred pairs in Taiwan
and left nine other pairs there in the care of local
aviculturists to produce further birds for release.

The Mikado Pheasant (*Syrmaticus mikado*) is also
found in Taiwan. Possibly only a few hundred now
survive in the wild, for like the former pheasant,
hunting pressure is causing the decline of this species.
The captive stock of the Mikado Pheasant is far
smaller than that of the Swinhoe's Pheasant, but it is
hoped that some birds from the Pheasant Trust will
eventually be sent back to Taiwan for release.

The magnificent Monkey-eating Eagle is in grave danger of extinction, for its total population may be only 40 birds

As we know only too well, there have been troubles in Vietnam for many years now. While this region of South East Asia remains in turmoil the status of the closely related Imperial Pheasant (*Lophura imperialis*) and Edward's Pheasant (*Lophura edwardsi*) will continue to be unknown. It is likely, however, that both are scarce. Edward's Pheasant was discovered in 1895, and in 1923 the Imperial Pheasant was the last pheasant to be discovered. Captive breeding stocks of both these species are low and very much in need of fresh blood.

The Japanese or Manchurian Crane (*Grus japonensis*) is showing signs of making a slight recovery after having become alarmingly scarce. This fine predominantly black and white crane was formerly found over a much wider range than it is today; its breeding grounds are in eastern Siberia and Japan. It figures largely in Japanese legend, folk-lore, history, and superstition; for example, it is considered a sign of forthcoming good luck and long life if it should visit a Japanese farmer's land. In Japan this species is fully protected, having been designated a national monument by the Japanese government in 1935, and has bred in confinement; a third of the world's population may be in zoos.

As man becomes ever more and more concerned at the plight of wildlife and creates more national parks and reserves, there is hope that many birds will be saved from possible extinction or scarcity. Such refuges help to provide areas where species can live and reproduce with the minimum of interference from human beings and perhaps, also, their domestic animals. Habitats conducive to the existence of certain species may be preserved or encouraged by allowing vegetation which gives cover or food to flourish, or by maintaining stretches of water or marsh by artificial means. Often predators are controlled, and man-made nesting places may be provided if enough natural ones do not exist. The part reserves or refuges can play in the future of a species is amply demonstrated by the dramatic increase of the Trumpeter Swan in the American Red Rock Lakes National Wildlife Refuge.

Another hope is in the breeding of endangered species in captivity. With modern methods of management, many species now breed far more successfully than ever before in confinement. Soon it may be possible to return numbers of captive-bred species to the wild to reinforce depleted wild stocks, as has already happened in the case of Swinhoe's Pheasant. Once some of the other species now breeding in confinement breed in sufficient numbers, they will also be able to be returned to the wild.

Unfortunately, not all species can be persuaded to reproduce in captivity. This is particularly true of birds of prey, a group of birds dwindling in population throughout the world. Some, like the cranes, do not successfully rear their full clutch even when living in the wild and part of it can be taken away and reared artificially. The artificially reared birds can either be retained to build a captive breeding stock or be released to swell the wild stock. If the egg or eggs are removed from the nest of many birds, they will often lay again. If the single egg of the California Condor were to be collected, then hatched and reared artificially, the condor might then lay a replacement and this would greatly increase its chances of survival.

An outstanding example of how captive-bred birds can save a species from impending extinction is the Hawaiian Goose or Nene (*Branta sandvicensis*). At one time thousands roamed the lowlands of Hawaii itself and could also be found on the neighbouring island of Maui. By 1900, however, the Nene had become rare even in the mountainous areas of Hawaii and on Maui had probably disappeared altogether. Fifty years later, man together with his introduced dogs and pigs, and perhaps also the introduced mongoose, had reduced the number to about fifty.

The first Nenes to reach Europe arrived in 1823, and were sent to a private menagerie belonging to Lord Derby. These first birds soon began to breed regularly. London Zoo received a pair in 1832 which bred two years later and continued to breed and raise young for several years. Soon they were distributed among many European zoos and private collections, although these establishments were unaware of the Nene's rapidly declining status in the wild. By 1910 only a few very old and inbred pairs remained. A male Nene which died or disappeared during the German invasion of France in 1940, for instance, was known to have been reared in Holland forty-two years before.

Early in 1950 two Nenes from Pohakuloa, Hawaii, arrived at the Wildfowl Trust at Slimbridge, England. The next year a gander was acquired when the first two birds both laid eggs. The gander was named Kamehameha after a great Hawaiian king. Nine young were reared at Slimbridge from the trio the following year. By the time that Kamehameha died, twelve years later, he was the ancestor of more than 230 birds. The Nenes were now breeding so well at Slimbridge that it was possible to return fifty birds to the wild to restock the island of Maui. In the meantime, a breeding stock had also been built up at Pohakuloa and was being used to restock Hawaii itself. By 1962 the total population of wild and captive geese was estimated to be 427. Four years later, more birds from Slimbridge were released on Maui and the world population was then over 500. As a safeguard against disease, parasites or other hazards, the captive stock is now dispersed among zoos and waterfowl collections all over the world. The Nene is Hawaii's state bird and is now fully protected.

Other endangered Hawaiian waterfowl are the Hawaiian Mallard or Koloa (*Anas platyrhynchos wyvilliana*) and the Laysan Teal (*Anas platyrhynchos laysanensis*). The present status of the Koloa is fairly good and it is in no immediate danger. In 1964 there was an estimated world population of about 500 birds of which sixty or seventy were in zoos or private collections. Unlike the Nene and Laysan Teal, however, it has not taken so readily to breeding in captivity.

The Laysan Teal lives on the small island of Laysan towards the remote western end of the Hawaiian archipelago. Although the population of this species seems to have fluctuated greatly through the years since the 1950s, it has been increasing. A count in 1957 revealed between 400 and 600 birds, yet in 1911 there were thought to be no more than six birds. The rabbit had been introduced on to Laysan

Today the Hawaiian Goose or Nene is probably no longer in danger of extinction, thanks to captive breeding programmes in Hawaii and at the Wildfowl Trust at Slimbridge in England

The Hawaiian Mallard or Koloa had an estimated world population of about 500 birds in 1964

A number of Swinhoe's Pheasants bred in
captivity at the Pheasant Trust in Norfolk
were recently released in Taiwan
to augment its diminishing wild stock

right
The Takahe, thought to be extinct, was
rediscovered on the South Island
of New Zealand in 1948

The Manchurian or Japanese Crane has
become alarmingly scarce; its breeding
grounds are in eastern Siberia and Japan

The last haunts of the Kakapo
or Owl Parrot are in beech forests
in remote areas of New Zealand

near the beginning of the present century and, before being eliminated there, had destroyed virtually all of the ground vegetation which provided cover for the teal. With the disappearance of the rabbit, the cover began to grow again and the teal started its upward climb. Since 1957 and 1958 when a number were distributed to the Wildfowl Trust, zoos and other waterfowl collections, it has continued to breed very well in captivity. In 1964 it was estimated that there were about 500 Laysan Teal in the wild.

The one species of goose and the two ducks now seem to be safe, but some of the smaller Hawaiian birds are still in danger of extinction, particularly one unique family of birds which have such names as Amakihi, Anianian, Nukupuu, Ou and Ula-ai-hawaul. Of the twenty-two species of Hawaiian Honeycreepers (*Drepanidiae*) eight have already disappeared, and eight other species, together with some races, are considered to be endangered.

New Zealand, like Hawaii, has a number of species in danger of vanishing altogether. A few like the rediscovered Takahe appear to be holding their own under strict protection. Some, like the Piopio or Native Thrush (*Turnagra capensis*) and the New Zealand Laughing Owl (*Sceloglaux albifacies*) are thought to be extremely rare. Discovered on Captain Cook's second voyage to New Zealand, the New Zealand Shore Plover (*Thinornis novaeseelandiae*) once occurred on both the North and South Island. Now it is probably just confined to Rangatira in the Chatham Islands, where it is breeding quite successfully. Fortunately, introduced cats and rats which have done so much damage to a large part of New Zealand's avifauna are absent from Rangatira.

Introduced predators, particularly stoats, along with forest clearance have done much to reduce the population of the strange, almost flightless Kakapo or Owl Parrot (*Strigops habroptilis*). A nocturnal species, it remains hidden during the day in rock crevices or burrows. The Kakapo's last haunts in New Zealand are in beech forests in relatively inaccessible and seldom visited areas. In Australia another nocturnal ground-living species, the Night Parrot (*Geopsittacus occidentalis*), has not been seen since 1937, the year in which it was given total protection, and may or may not still exist. Just under a hundred years ago it was quite widely distributed, being found in central Australia, northern South Australia and inland Western Australia, and probably also western Queensland and western New South Wales.

On the island of New Caledonia, halfway between Australia and Fiji lives a quaint-looking bird called the Kagu (*Rhynochetos jubatus*). This unique bird is placed in a sub-family of its own, close to the cranes and rails. Found only on New Caledonia, the Kagu was at one time widespread, but now lives a precarious existence in the more remote mountainous areas. It is principally a nocturnal bird and lives on the forest floor, rarely flying. Worms, insects and other small animal life form its diet. The Kagu is now fully protected by law and a scheme to turn part of its natural habitat into a reserve is now being considered.

A Spanish Imperial Eagle at its nest.
It has recently been estimated that the
species now numbers only about 100 birds.

far left
The Laughing Owl of New Zealand
may now be extinct

left
The unique Kagu, which is placed in
a subfamily of its own close to
the cranes and rails, lives only
on the island of New Caledonia
in the Pacific Ocean

Bird Artists and their Work

The most famous of all bird artists is undoubtedly John James Audubon. He is known for his splendid pictures of North American birds, which he drew while travelling about America in the early nineteenth century. Audubon developed his passion for nature in the countryside around Nantes in France, where he was brought up. He studied art in Paris and when he was eighteen his father sent him to America. In 1808 he married and with his wife set out to explore America and portray its wildlife. In order to obtain a living he worked at many businesses, without much success, and began to accumulate a considerable number of bird drawings. In time he decided to have his work reproduced and published. Realizing that there was no one in America capable of reproducing it to the standard he required, he sailed from New Orleans for England with his work in 1826. His 435 pictures illustrated *Birds of America* which was published in London in four huge volumes between 1827 and 1838. The enormous size of the plates is because the birds were represented life-size. It is now rare to find a complete set of *Birds of America* and recently at a Sotheby auction a record price of £90,000 was paid for such a work in good condition. After the publication of these volumes, Audubon returned to America to carry on drawing. He died in New York on 27th January, 1851.

Audubon's English rival was the remarkable scientist and artist, John Gould. From the early 1830s until his death in 1881, Gould was responsible for a tremendous number of illustrated folios, notes, papers and scientific memoirs. The first of his famous series of illustrated folio works, *A Century of Birds of the Himalaya Mountains,* appeared in 1832. In the preparation of the lithographic plates for all his works, Gould was assisted by a team which included his wife, Edward Lear, H. C. Richter, Joseph Wolf, and others. Gould's father became a gardener at Windsor Castle when the artist was in his early teens, and it was at Windsor that he developed his interest in birds. Joseph Wolf, who joined Gould in 1848, later became a popular artist.

The first great bird artist of the twentieth century, as well as the last of the nineteenth, was Archibald Thorburn. He was born 31st May, 1860 at Lasswade in Midlothian near Edinburgh, the fifth son of the famous miniaturist Robert Thorburn. His first work was published in 1883. Thorburn painted chiefly British birds, and was equally skilled in his portrayal of both large and small birds. His illustrations for Lord Lilford's *Coloured Figures of the Birds of the British Isles* may well be the most widely reproduced bird pictures of all time, for they still appear in modern editions of T. A. Coward's *Birds of the British Isles.* After the First World War Thorburn settled at Hascombe, Godalming, Surrey, and died there in October, 1935. Today examples of his work are in great demand, and an original Thorburn is a collector's piece. Recently the fine plates from his great four-volume work *British Birds* were brought out as a single volume entitled *Thorburn's Birds.* This single volume which contains eighty-two plates has been edited by James Fisher, who has also written a new text in place of Thorburn's own.

Gold and Blue Macaw
by Axel Amuchastegui.
In the collection of
Mrs Constance Mellon Byers.

Gyrfalcon by David Reid-Henry.
From *Eagles, Hawks and Falcons of the World* by Leslie Brown and Dean Amadon.

Roseate, Sandwich, Arctic, Common
and Little Terns. From *British Birds*
by Archibald Thorburn.

Roseate Tern.

Arctic Tern.

Common Tern.

Sandwich Tern.

Little Tern.

Yellowhammer.
From *The Birds of Great Britain*
by John Gould.

Blue Magpie.
From *The Birds of Asia* by John Gould.

Roseate Spoonbill. From *The Birds of America* by John James Audubon.

left
Pheasant. Detail from a painting
by Archibald Thorburn.
Private collection.

G. E. Lodge, the celebrated bird artist,
in his studio

left
Gyrfalcon by G. E. Lodge

Another outstanding bird artist born in the same
year as Thorburn was George Lodge. Lodge became
a keen falconer at a very early age, and it was in the
painting of falcons that he excelled. He worked right
up until the time he died at the age of ninety-three.
Unfortunately, he only lived to see the publication of
the first volume of *The Birds of the British Isles,*
which he illustrated to accompany David
Bannerman's text. George Lodge preferred to paint in
tempera or oils, whereas Thorburn rarely used oils
and preferred water-colours.

An artist to whom Lodge gave much valuable
encouragement is David Reid-Henry, who has
progressed to become one of today's most outstanding
painters of birds. His pictures of birds from all parts
of the world are perfect in every detail. He was born
in Ceylon in 1919, the son of George Henry, an author
and illustrator of many ornithological works
including *Birds of Ceylon.* David Reid-Henry has
painted illustrations for many books and journals,
including a number of fine plates for *Eagles, Hawks
and Falcons of the World* by Brown and Amadon.

Among the present day bird artists in the United
States, the most notable are Roger Tory Peterson,
Arthur Singer, and Don R. Eckelberry. Roger Tory
Peterson is best known for his illustrations in field

guides to North America and European birds. He has also won wide acclaim as an ornithologist, writer, and photographer. Arthur Singer illustrated *Birds of the World,* and more recently *British & European Birds in colour* by Bertel Bruun. Eckelberry has illustrated among other books James Bond's *Birds of the West Indies.* It was from this book that the late Ian Fleming, who had a home on Jamaica and was interested in the island's birds, took the author's name for his world-famous character. Eckelberry specializes in North and Central American birds, which he paints mainly in water-colours.

Another outstanding artist in North America is J. Fenwick Lansdowne. Born in Hong Kong of British parents who later moved to Canada, he became interested in birds at an early age. His first exhibition was held in the Royal Ontario Museum in Toronto when he was only nineteen. Since then he has exhibited his fine paintings at major galleries in North America and England. His work is represented in many famous collections, including the private collection of Prince Philip, Duke of Edinburgh.

In his pictures of birds Axel Amuchastegui paints every feather, every branch, and every piece of foliage in the most unbelievable detail. His work is of such high quality that it is in great demand and brings high prices. When he last held an exhibition in London, all his paintings were sold within a few hours of the opening. Because of their high prices, his paintings are not as well known to the general public as the work of some lesser artists.

Born in Argentina in 1921, he worked for many years as a commercial artist in advertising. In the past he also painted an enormous variety of other subjects in many mediums before finally concentrating on wildlife. Among wildlife artists he is rather unusual in having come to birds through his art rather than his subject. Amuchastegui paints his wonderfully detailed pictures in Chinese inks, not using a pen as might be expected, but with a brush. As a preliminary, he makes many pencil drawings from skins, his own coloured photographs and from rough sketches made during field trips. His chief subject matter is the bird life of his native South America, but he is equally skilled at portraying its mammals.

Chloe Talbot Kelly, Rena Fennessy, and the late Winifred Austen, are the only women to have achieved prominence as bird painters. Winifred Austen, who died a few years ago, studied and painted the wildlife of the English countryside in which she lived. She possessed the gift of being able to paint the creatures she knew so well in their natural surroundings, and to capture some of their individual characteristics. Chloe Talbot Kelly is best known for her illustrations in books and journals. Anybody who has visited East Africa in the past few years must be familiar with the bird paintings of Rena Fennessy, for there can be very few hotels or game lodges without at least one print of her work. A resident of Kenya, she has a wealth of glossy starlings, sunbirds, and many other lovely birds to paint.

Other notable bird artists include Peter Scott, Roland Green, J. C. Harrison, the Frenchman Paul Barruel, and the Australian Robin Hill.

Grey Herons and Purple Heron by Arthur Singer. From *British and European Birds in Colour* by Bertel Bruun.

Indian Griffon or Long-billed Vulture,
Indian White-backed Vulture and
Himalayan Griffon by Roger Tory Peterson.
From *Eagles, Hawks and Falcons of the
World* by Leslie Brown and Dean Amadon.

Orange-headed Marsh Bird
by Axel Amuchastegui

Kookaburra by Robin Hill

Snipe in winter's grip by J. C. Harrison

Pied Wagtails by J. F. Lansdowne

Acknowledgements

Colour

A.F.A. Ltd. 103; British Museum (Natural History) 130; Hamlyn Group Library 131 bottom; Ingmar Holmåsen 74; Eric Hosking 52, 99 bottom; Frank Lane 20 top, 20 bottom left, 21, 45, 56, 60, 75 top, 98, 99 top; John Markham 44 bottom; New Zealand Wildlife Service 122 bottom; Photo Researchers jacket, 17, 24, 40, 44 top, 49, 53, 78, 83; David Reid-Henry 126; Sotheby and Co. 131 top; W. Suschitzky 16; Maurice Tibbles – Wildlife Photos 123; Tierbilder Okapia 57; The Tryon Gallery 127; John Warham 75 bottom, 102; Philip Wayre 122 top; Z.F.A. 20 bottom right, 37, 41, 79, 82, 107.

Black and white

Australian News and Information Bureau 27 right, 73 top; British Museum (Natural History) 10, 11, 12 top, 12 bottom, 14 bottom, 15; Allan D. Cruickshank: from National Audubon Society 116; Malcolm Ellis 84 top; Dr. B. Grzimek 91 bottom; Ingmar Holmåsen Half-title, 46, 55 bottom, 58; Eric Hosking 35 top, 43 top, 48, 50 top, 50 bottom, 51, 63 bottom, 81 top, 84 bottom, 85 bottom left, 85 bottom right, 86 bottom, 87 top left, 90-91 top, 92 top, 94, 96, 100, 105 bottom, 108 bottom right, 111 right, 125 top; Frank Lane 29 left, 32 bottom, 33 top, 34, 38 bottom, 54 top, 69 top right, 70 top, 72 bottom, 80 bottom right, 85 top, 88, 97 bottom left, 113, 121 bottom; John Markham 59 top, 61 bottom, 97 bottom right; New Zealand Wildlife Service 125 bottom left; Tierbilder Okapia 14 top, 22, 26 top, 62, 63 top, 69 top left, 73 bottom, 80 bottom left, 87 bottom, 89, 90 bottom, 125 bottom right; R. T. Peterson 136; Popperfoto 26 bottom, 36 centre right, 65, 68, 104 top, 108 bottom left; Photo Researchers Frontispiece, 13 top, 18 top, 19, 23, 27 left, 29 right, 30, 31, 32 top, 33 bottom, 35 bottom, 36 top, 38 top, 39 top, 39 bottom, 47, 55 top, 59 bottom, 61 top, 70 bottom, 71 top, 71 bottom, 72 top, 76, 77, 80 top, 81 bottom left, 81 bottom right, 86 top, 87 top right, 92 bottom, 95, 97 top, 101, 105 top, 109 top, 109 centre, 109 bottom, 110, 111 left, 112 bottom, 114, 115 left, 115 right, 119 bottom, 121 top, 124; Pictorial Press 13 bottom; Radio Times Hulton Picture Library 117, 118, 119 top, 129; George Rainbird, Ltd. 128; A. Singer, 135; W. Suschitzky Endpapers, 18 bottom, 36 bottom, 42 left, 42 right, 67, 106 bottom, 108 top, 120; The Tryon Gallery 132, 133, 137, 138 top, 138 bottom, 139; John Warham 54 bottom, 66, 69 centre left, 69 bottom, 104 bottom, 106 top, 112 top; Zoological Society of London 38 centre, 43 bottom.